IT STARTS WITH YOU

*Guidelines for Her
Personal Happiness and
a Successful Love Relationship*

Julia J. Austin

Copyright © 2004 by Julia J. Austin.

Illustrations by Bob Jackie

Library of Congress Number:		2003095740
ISBN :	Hardcover	1-4134-2623-9
	Softcover	1-4134-2622-0

All rights reserved. No part of this book may be reproduced or transmitted in any form or by any means, electronic or mechanical, including photocopying, recording, or by any information storage and retrieval system, without permission in writing from the copyright owner.

This book was printed in the United States of America.

To order additional copies of this book, contact:
Xlibris Corporation
1-888-795-4274
www.Xlibris.com
Orders@Xlibris.com
19024

CONTENTS

Acknowledgments IX
Introduction XI
Preface XIII

SECTION ONE
HOW TO BE THE RIGHT PERSON

Chapter 1: What Is My Is My Starting Point? 1
Chapter 2: Love Yourself 11
Chapter 3: Take Care Of Yourself 19
Chapter 4: A Better You 29
Introduction To Sections Two And Three 52

SECTION TWO
HOW TO FIND THE RIGHT PERSON

Chapter 5: A Few Pointers 56
Chapter 6: Watch Your Behavior 61

SECTION THREE
HOW TO DETERMINE IF HE IS
THE RIGHT PERSON FOR YOU

Chapter 7: Getting Serious 66
Chapter 8: Determine If You Are Compatible 68
Chapter 9: If He's Not The "One" 99

SECTION FOUR
HOW TO MAKE IT LAST A LIFETIME

Chapter 10: Mates For Life 103
Chapter 11: Keeping The Romance Alive 127

Reference Guide 133
Appendix 1: Recommended Books,
    Audio Tapes and Video Tapes 135
Appendix 2: Bible references 157
Appendix 3: Supporting Documentation 172
Appendix 4: Contact Information 227
Appendix 5: Credits 235
Index 239

This book is dedicated to my daughter
who died in infancy and to my five nieces,
and most of all, it is dedicated to the Glory of God.

Acknowledgments

I would like to acknowledge my husband, my son, and my many friends who encouraged me to write this book and supported me in doing so. Without their support and encouragement, this book would not have been possible.

Introduction

I do not like long introductions, so I will make this short and to the point. I have had several relationships with men that did not work out for one reason or another. I am now in the fifteenth year of a healthy, mutually satisfying relationship that I have every reason to believe will last a lifetime.

As a result of my experiences in life, I have come to the conclusion that a successful, healthy, long-term relationship is comprised of two main parts. The first part is being the right person and the second part is finding the right person for you.

This book is comprised of guidelines divided into four parts. The first part will help you become the right person (if you aren't already). The second part will help you attract members of the opposite sex. After you have established a relationship with a man, the third part will help you to determine if he is the right person for you. The fourth part will help you make the relationship last a lifetime.

It is also my hope that this book will be helpful to those already in a long-term relationship. In that case, the first part will help you become a better partner. (You can skip the second part since you are already in a relationship with a man.) The third part will help you determine if you have chosen the right person for you. The fourth part will help you to make it last a lifetime.

This is *not* intended to be a rulebook. It is merely guidelines designed to help you establish a healthy, mutually satisfying relationship that has the best chance of lasting a lifetime.

Preface

When I was a young girl I used to think that the most important thing in my life was to grow up and get married. Somewhere I got the notion that unless I had a man in my life, I would be nothing. I believed my purpose in life was to be the perfect wife. I was caught up in all those fairy tales about the handsome prince rescuing (in one form or another) the young maiden and the two of them living "happily ever after."

My family was dysfunctional and my childhood was unhappy. I couldn't wait to get old enough to find my "handsome prince" who would rescue me from my unhappy circumstances. I thought that if I could just find a man to marry me, everything would be fine, and I would be happy for the rest of my life.

At age seventeen, and just two weeks after high school graduation, I left home and moved to the city where my boyfriend lived. My boyfriend and I married about one year later. When we married, we had known each other just over two years.

We started dating when I was sixteen and he was twenty-two. The courtship was a stormy one, to say the least. I broke up with him several times because there were so many problems between us. Somehow, he always talked me into taking him back. He would promise things would be different and I would believe him. Things would be different, for a while, and then it would go back to the way it was before.

Deep in my heart, I knew this relationship couldn't work, but he said he loved me (and I needed so desperately to be loved), so I overlooked all of the danger signs.

During my spring break from college, we eloped. I recall standing in front of the preacher with my husband-to-be at my side. As I recited the vows, there was a voice in my head saying, "Why are you doing this? You know it won't work!" I ignored the voice in my head, and committed myself to a relationship that was doomed from the beginning.

That marriage lasted just over one year. I married him out of guilt and because I felt sorry for him. Neither were good reasons on which to build a lifetime relationship. I filed for divorce and when it was final (three months later) I moved to another state. So much for marriage number one.

I resolved to start over again, fresh, in a new place where no one knew me. The problem was I was still the same person. I hadn't yet learned from my mistakes, so I was destined to repeat them.

And repeat them I did! My second serious relationship was with a man who was heavily into drugs and alcohol. I overlooked his problem because he was so likeable and charming. We were common-law married, and were together for about a year. Then he got a job transfer and moved to another state. I put in for a job transfer so we could be together. Three months later, my transfer went through and I thought we would finally have a formal wedding ceremony.

The day I showed up at my "husband's" new place of employment, a terrible shock was waiting for me. Even though we had been common-law married for a year, and he had promised to have an official wedding ceremony, he had a "date" with another woman! He assured me this was only his last "fling" before we had our wedding. A few weeks later, this other woman had moved in with him!

He ended up having his wedding with her instead of me. I was heartbroken, but I later realized that he did me a favor. However, at the time I still didn't see what was wrong with me and I couldn't understand why my relationships kept falling apart.

About six years passed between that relationship and my next committed relationship. During that time, I had one "dating" relationship after another, each lasting anywhere from a few weeks to several months. Also during that time, I started to realize that maybe I needed to make some changes in myself, so I began to see counselors and get therapy.

The therapy helped, but I was still not a "whole" person by the time I met the next man with whom I would have a committed relationship. I had joined the U.S. Air Force and was stationed far from home. At the church I attended, I met this handsome, outgoing, debonair, young man who seemed to me to be the most wonderful man I had ever met! I guess you could say he "swept me off my feet." He was in the U.S. Army and said he wanted to be a preacher when he got out of the army. I found that to be very appealing.

He proposed only two weeks after we met and I said "yes." I could see myself as a preacher's wife, and thought if I married someone who was going to be a preacher, surely the marriage would last. We had known each other only one month by the time we married. As soon as we were married, we moved into a one-bedroom apartment in the town where we were both stationed in the military.

We were both very involved in church activities and I thought that at last I had found my "handsome prince." But, alas, even though this relationship did last longer than the previous ones I was involved with, it also was doomed to failure.

You see, I did not invest the time necessary to really get to know him before we got married. Also, I married him for the wrong reasons, i.e., guilt and fear. This marriage lasted four years and left me with a six-month-old son to care for on my own.

My next "adventure" in marriage began when my son

was two years old. I tried to rekindle a relationship with a former boyfriend. He thought it was better for us to be just "friends" and subsequently introduced me to his older brother. I still wanted to be with the younger brother who was tall and handsome. His older brother was the "runt" of the family, and I felt sorry for him. But because the two brothers usually double-dated, I thought that if I dated the older brother, I could be in the company of the younger brother I really wanted to be with. I know, you are probably saying to yourself, "Boy, this lady was really screwed up," and you would be right. In spite of all I had been through so far, I still had not figured out what I needed to do to change myself so I could be a whole person. I was still looking for a man to make me complete in some way. It's too bad I had never heard the quote from Anais Nin which says, "How wrong it is for a woman to expect the man to build the world she wants, rather than to create it herself."

After a year or so of dating, I married the older brother. This man who was the "runt" of the family seemed to need me, and I honestly thought to myself, "If I don't marry him, it's likely no one else will. He will appreciate me so much for marrying him, that it will make me feel complete." His younger brother was the best man at our wedding. I remember thinking to myself on my wedding day, "Yeah; he really is the 'best' man." What an idiot I was! I was marrying one man so I could be near the one I really loved. What was I thinking?

It wasn't long before this "rescue" relationship started wearing thin. I discovered that my new husband hated children and only "tolerated" my son because he wanted to be with me. I also discovered that he exhibited obsessive-compulsive behavior, and had an extremely negative outlook on life. I sought out professional help and my husband and I started seeing a marriage and family counselor. After just a few sessions, the counselor was able to determine that we were sitting on a "ticking time bomb" just waiting to explode.

It finally dawned on me that this marriage was not right from the beginning. Another revelation was soon to come. While my husband and I were watching a program on TV about drug addiction, he started to cry. He confessed to me that he was a cocaine addict and an alcoholic.

After that, I started to go to Al-Anon meetings and he started to go to Alcoholics Anonymous meetings. However, the more meetings I attended the more I realized just how sick our relationship was and I had to get out for the sake of both of us.

I came home from an Al-Anon meeting one evening and told my husband, "I don't love you, and I have never loved you, and I don't think I can ever love you." At that point, he said that if that was the case, there was no point in staying together. He moved out shortly thereafter and filed for divorce.

One thing that Al-Anon taught me is that I am not responsible for any other adult. By this time I also realized that being happy in life wasn't about finding a man to make everything all right for me, and it wasn't about "fixing" someone else either. I discovered that if I ever hoped to find the "right" man for me, I had to first "fix" myself and make sure I was a complete person before I could expect to find a man with whom to build a lifetime relationship.

I resolved to change my attitudes, get my own act together and do whatever was necessary so I wouldn't keep making the same mistakes in my choices of men. This took time, counseling, Bible study and a lot of prayer. I read several self-help books, sought out Christian counselors for guidance and spent many hours searching and meditating on the Scriptures. As a result of my realizations and the changes that subsequently occurred, I was able cast off a lot of my old "baggage" and put myself in a better place mentally and emotionally to attract the right man.

It was while I was pursuing my goal to further my education that the right man was attracted to me. We became friends first. That friendship blossomed into love that eventually led to marriage. We are soul mates and are still very much in love after more than fifteen years.

It is upon my experiences that this book is based. It is the "wrong choices" I have made in life that have given me the valuable experience necessary to change myself and then it was possible for me to make the right choices that led to a happy relationship.

I am opening up my heart and sharing what I have learned from my mistakes in hopes of preventing you from making the same mistakes in your life. I also hope that I can serve as an example that it is possible to change from a negative attitude to a positive attitude, and one can turn failure into success. I also want you to understand that just because you may not be where you want to be in your life right now, that doesn't mean you have to stay there.

When I was a teenager, I saw a quote in the newspaper. It said, "We should learn from others' mistakes because we can't possibly live long enough to make them all ourselves," (Author Unknown). If just one of you reading this book can learn from the mistakes I have made and benefit from the positive changes in my life thus improving your own life because of it, I will have accomplished my objective.

You see, it is easy to realize when someone else is making a mistake. It is much more difficult to see when we are making a mistake ourselves. So, please read this book with an open mind and open heart and a willingness to change. And most of all, be honest with yourself. By doing so, you will save yourself a lot of grief and heartache in your life.

SECTION ONE

HOW TO BE
THE RIGHT PERSON

Chapter 1

What Is My Starting Point?

My life experiences taught me the first step in building a successful, mutually satisfying, long-term relationship is laying the foundation. It is my belief that where to begin is with yourself. It is important to prepare yourself to be the best person you can be and enter into a relationship from a position of strength rather than a position of weakness. A healthy relationship is not two "halves" making a "whole" but rather two "whole" people joining together to make an equal partnership.

It is important to be honest with yourself and do a self-assessment to make sure you are a "whole" person yourself *before* you think about entering into a long-term relationship with a man. What I mean by "whole" person is: someone who is emotionally and mentally healthy; someone who has a healthy self-esteem and is self-confident, and someone with a healthy outlook on life who knows where she is going and what is important to her. In short, someone who is complete or "whole" by herself.

The following questionnaire may help you determine how complete you are and where you may need to make some improvements.

HOW DO I FEEL ABOUT MYSELF?

Please answer the following questions "true" or "false" as they pertain to you. Be as honest as possible. This will only be helpful to you if you are honest in your response.

1. Basically, I believe I am a good person.
TRUE   FALSE

2. I am happy with myself most of the time.
TRUE   FALSE

3. I feel good about how my body looks.
TRUE   FALSE

4. When I look in the mirror, I like what I see.
TRUE   FALSE

5. I need others to approve of me in order to feel good about myself.
TRUE   FALSE

6. Most of the time, I do what I feel is right regardless of what others may think.
TRUE   FALSE

Is This You?

"I'm happy with myself most of the time."

7. I often feel that I am worthless as a person.
TRUE   FALSE

8. I wish I had a prettier face.
TRUE   FALSE

9. I think that I am overweight more than just a little.
TRUE   FALSE

10. It is easy for me to make friends.
TRUE   FALSE

11. I need a man in my life to feel complete.
TRUE   FALSE

12. I consider myself to be an honest person.
TRUE   FALSE

13. I often wish I had never been born.
TRUE   FALSE

14. Most people like me.
TRUE   FALSE

15. I am afraid to let anyone know who I really am for fear that person would not like me.
TRUE   FALSE

16. If I had to, I could be happy being single the rest of my life.
TRUE   FALSE

17. It is easy for me to express myself.
TRUE   FALSE

18. I think I am less attractive than most women.
TRUE   FALSE

19. I would do anything just to be with a man.
TRUE   FALSE

20. I think I have a lot to offer to the world.
TRUE   FALSE

21. I think I have a pretty face.
TRUE   FALSE

22. I have the need to be needed.
TRUE   FALSE

23. I think I am attractive.
TRUE   FALSE

24. I feel I can take care of myself, and I don't need a man to do that for me.
TRUE   FALSE

25. I am in reasonably good health.
TRUE   FALSE

26. I believe that my spirit is eternal and will live forever.
TRUE   FALSE

27. Making friends is difficult for me.
TRUE   FALSE

28. I feel I need a man to rescue me.
TRUE   FALSE

29. I generally trust people unless they give me a reason not to.
TRUE   FALSE

30. I often become so angry, I can't control my actions.
TRUE   FALSE

31. I believe in a power greater than myself.
TRUE   FALSE

32. I feel I need a man to take care of me.
TRUE   FALSE

33. When I am upset or stressed out, a few drinks always make me feel better.
TRUE   FALSE

34. I often lie to protect myself.
TRUE   FALSE

35. I think I was born into the world for a reason.
TRUE   FALSE

36. I seldom trust anyone.
TRUE   FALSE

37. When I am angry, I control myself.
TRUE   FALSE

38. I sometimes get so drunk, I don't remember what happened.
TRUE   FALSE

39. I don't feel sexy most of the time.
TRUE   FALSE

40. I find it difficult to express myself.
TRUE   FALSE

41. Most of the time, I eat a balanced diet.
TRUE   FALSE

42. I have the need to take care of a man.
TRUE   FALSE

43. I believe that drugs or alcohol, or both, are an acceptable way to escape the pressures of life.
TRUE   FALSE

44. I am in reasonably good physical condition.
TRUE   FALSE

45. I often eat "junk food."
TRUE   FALSE

46. I know where I am going and what I want out of life.
TRUE   FALSE

47. When I am right, I stand up for myself.
TRUE   FALSE

48. I don't believe in "life after death."
TRUE   FALSE

49. I am often unhappy with who I am.
TRUE   FALSE

50. I believe someone other than me is controlling my mind.
TRUE   FALSE

51. Most of the time, I look forward to each new day.
TRUE   FALSE

52. People often talk about me behind my back.
TRUE   FALSE

53. I often eat something in order to make my self feel good, whether I am hungry or not.
TRUE   FALSE

54. I understand that I am the one who is responsible for where I am in my life right now.
TRUE   FALSE

55. My weight is in proportion to my height and bone structure.
TRUE   FALSE

56. I am in control of my thoughts and my actions.
TRUE   FALSE

57. I take responsibility for my choices in life.
TRUE   FALSE

58. I seldom stand up for myself.
TRUE   FALSE

59. Most of the time, I only eat when I am hungry and I stop when I am full.
TRUE   FALSE

60. Most of the time, I am afraid of what the future holds for me.
TRUE   FALSE

61. When I look in the mirror, I don't like what I see.
TRUE   FALSE

62. Most of the time, I am glad to be alive.
TRUE   FALSE

63. I believe I need to be with a man to be happy in life.
TRUE   FALSE

64. I am not afraid to reveal who I am to someone I feel close to.
TRUE   FALSE

65. I would never compromise my beliefs or my dignity in order to be with a man.
TRUE   FALSE

66. I don't believe in a God or Supreme Being of any kind.
TRUE   FALSE

67. I want a man who can take care of himself.
TRUE   FALSE

68. Most of the time, I think I am a bad person.
TRUE   FALSE

69. I think I am sexy.
TRUE   FALSE

70. I believe that drinking alcohol is *not* the best way to relieve stress.
TRUE   FALSE

71. I am in poor health.
TRUE   FALSE

72. I am not responsible for the choices I make.
TRUE   FALSE

73. I don't need a man to rescue me.
TRUE   FALSE

74. I don't like how my body looks.
TRUE   FALSE

75. I do not need a man in my life to make me feel complete.
TRUE   FALSE

76. I am in poor physical condition.
TRUE   FALSE

77. I don't have the need to be needed.
TRUE   FALSE

78. I don't believe there is a purpose for my life.
TRUE   FALSE

79. I am sick a lot of the time.
TRUE   FALSE

80. I have never gotten so drunk that I didn't remember what happened.
TRUE   FALSE

81. I don't know where I am going, or what I want out of life.
TRUE   FALSE

82. I don't believe I need drugs or alcohol to escape the pressures of life.
TRUE   FALSE

83. It is someone else's fault that I am where I am in my life right now.
TRUE   FALSE

84. I am rarely sick.
TRUE   FALSE

Is this you?

"I don't know where I am going, or what I want out of life."

HOW TO SCORE YOUR ANSWERS

The following questions come from a positive frame of reference. We will refer to this as "Group A":

1   6   16   23   29   41   51   57   65   73   82

2	10	17	24	31	44	54	59	67	75	84
3	12	20	25	35	46	55	62	69	77	
4	14	21	26	37	47	56	64	70	80	

In contrast to this, the following questions come from a negative frame of reference. We will refer to this group as "Group B":

5	11	19	30	36	42	49	58	66	74	81
7	13	22	32	38	43	50	60	68	76	83
8	15	27	33	39	45	52	61	71	78	
9	18	28	34	40	48	53	63	72	79	

Now, if you answered all or most of the questions in Group A, "TRUE" and all or most of the questions in Group B, "FALSE," then congratulations! You are most likely a fairly "together" person. You may want to take a closer look at any questions in Group A that you answered "FALSE" and any questions in Group B that you answered "TRUE." These may indicate areas in which you could improve yourself.

Please note, this is not meant as a comprehensive psychological test. It is meant only to give you an indication of what areas need improvement and where you may choose to start on a self-improvement program. If you have any serious personal issues that need attention, I recommend that you seek professional help. [1]

Now that you have an idea of what your starting point is, let's move on towards helping you be the right person. Feel free to skip any sections that you feel you have already mastered in your life.

Chapter 2

Love Yourself

The first point I would like to cover is loving yourself. If you are going to build a healthy, happy relationship with a man, you need to have a proper love for yourself. I'm not talking about self-centered love or a superiority complex here. The Bible tells us to "Love your neighbor as yourself." [2] If you don't know how to love yourself, you won't know how to love anyone else either.

I have to be honest with you; it has been very difficult and has taken me many years to learn how to have a proper love for myself. Personally, I feel our society does not really teach us much about how to love ourselves in the right way. The media offers us a very distorted view of what love really is. If you want to know how to love yourself, and subsequently how to love others, you have to go to another source.

In order to determine if you have the proper love for yourself, you need to understand something about what proper love is. The best description of proper love that I have ever found happens to be in the Bible. It is found in I Corinthians Chapter 13 verses 4-8. If you do not believe in the inspiration of the Scriptures, that's okay; this is still an excellent definition of love. "Love is patient, and love is kind. Love is not jealous; it does not boast, and it is not proud. Love is not rude; love is not selfish, and love does not become angry easily. Love does not remember wrongs done against it. Love is not happy with evil, but love is happy with the truth. Love patiently accepts all things. Love always trusts, always hopes, and always continues strong. Love never ends."

Let's examine each of these points one at a time. "Love is patient..." Are you patient with yourself? If you love yourself properly you will be patient with yourself. You will allow yourself the time necessary to learn and grow and improve yourself. You *won't* beat yourself up and get down on yourself because you're not a perfect person or because you don't learn things quickly enough.

"... Love is kind..." Are you kind to yourself? Do you treat yourself with the same honor and respect as the most important people in your life?

"Love is not jealous..." Have you learned how to master jealousy in your life? If you ever find yourself envying anyone else for any reason, this is an area for improvement.

"... It does not boast, and it is not proud." Do you know how to be humble? Can you gracefully accept recognition, without bragging about it and flaunting it? Humility is part of loving yourself.

"Love is not rude..." Those who are rude to others don't think very highly of themselves. Practice good manners and treat others with respect. This is one way of loving yourself properly.

"... Love is not selfish..." When you love yourself properly, you are not selfish. Thinking only of yourself and what you want is not the same thing as loving yourself. You are not alone in this world. You are part of a greater whole. If you truly love yourself, you will recognize this and put your wants and needs in proper prospective.

There is an unexpected pitfall in this area, however. Sometimes we can deceive ourselves into believing we are not being selfish by giving too much of ourselves to another person. We can think that the other person's needs are more important than our own; therefore we try to meet all of that person's needs and demands without regard to our own needs. Even though on the surface this appears to be selfless, it is in reality another form of selfishness. You see, the selfish need here is to fill our own emptiness by trying to be everything someone else needs. The voice in our head is saying, "If I am everything this person needs, then maybe that person will love me." This is selfishness in disguise.

". . . Love does not become angry easily . . ." This means not becoming easily angry with yourself. Cut yourself some slack. Don't say demeaning things to yourself. Don't get mad at yourself. Use the mistakes you make as a learning experience.

"Love does not remember wrongs done against it." Do you keep track of everything you have ever done wrong in your life and keep reminding yourself of all of those wrongs? If you do, then you do not love yourself properly. Let go of the past. Each new day you have the chance to start over and begin again. Don't limit your future by your past. Love yourself and forgive yourself and resolve to do better just one day at a time.

"Love is not happy with evil, but love is happy with the truth." Cultivate a positive outlook on life and dwell on those things that are right and true. When "bad" thoughts

> You can't keep the birds from flying over your head. . .
>
> but you can keep them from nesting in your hair!

come into your head, get rid of them immediately! My mother used to say, "You can't keep the birds from flying over your head, but you can keep them from nesting in your hair!" (To the best of my research, this quote is attributed to Martin Luther.)

The point is, we have control over our thoughts, and the thoughts we entertain, determine our actions. If you want to love yourself properly, work on controlling your thoughts and only allow those thoughts to remain in your head that will uplift you and help you to be a better person.

"Love patiently accepts all things." Do you patiently accept yourself just as you are? I am reminded of the "Serenity Prayer" that is taught in the "12-step" programs: "God, grant me the serenity to accept the things I cannot change, the courage to change the things I can, and the wisdom to know the difference." This does not mean you stop trying to improve yourself. It only means you love yourself enough to be accepting of who you are and where you are at any given moment on your journey through life.

"Love always trusts . . ." Do you trust yourself and your judgment? It is important for you to have confidence in yourself to the point that you trust the decisions you make in your life. If you doubt your own judgment or you aren't sure you can make a wise decision, then perhaps you need to work harder at loving yourself. I am reminded of a little story someone told me:

A young man, who was a bank teller in a bank, went to the president of the bank and said, "How do I get to be the president of the bank?"

The president replied, "By making the right decisions."

The young man inquired, "But how do I know how to make the right decisions?"

The president informed him, "Experience, my boy."

The young man was still puzzled. "But, sir, how do I get experience?"

The president answered, "By making the wrong decisions!"

I hope the point of this story is obvious. You don't need to make perfect decisions all of the time in order to trust yourself. Do the best you can with what you have at your disposal and if you make a mistake, learn from it and move on.

"... Always hopes..." Part of loving yourself is not letting anyone steal your hopes and dreams. I'm not talking about hopes and dreams that are an unrealistic fantasy. I'm talking about the hopes and dreams that inspire you, and lift you up to be the best person you can be. I'm talking about the kinds of hopes and dreams that the Wright Brothers had about making human flight a reality. I'm talking about the vision of Thomas Edison who brought us the electric light bulb. I'm talking about the dreams of a little girl to become the first woman astronaut. If you have a desire deep in your heart that you want to be true in your life, then loving yourself is not letting anyone take that away from you.

"... And always continues strong. Love never ends." Another word for this is steadfast. When you love yourself properly, it is not an on and off thing. It is constant... every moment of every day. It is loving yourself when you feel unlovable. It is understanding that even with all your weaknesses and shortcomings, you are still worthy of your own love.

When you begin to grasp what it is to truly love yourself in the proper way, then and only then will you be ready to open your heart and love a man in a way that will last a lifetime.

SELF-ESTEEM, CONFIDENCE AND SECURITY

The next subject I would like to talk about is self-esteem. In order to be a whole person it is important to have a healthy self-esteem. This is what you think of yourself and is definitely related to loving yourself. In our culture, quite often women are conditioned to have a very low self-esteem. It is important to examine how you feel about yourself and determine if you have a healthy self-esteem. If you feel as though you don't deserve all of the best that life has to offer, then this is most likely an indication that your self-esteem could stand some improvement.

In the previous self-evaluation, there are several questions that relate to self-esteem, confidence and security. Please check your answers again. If you answered questions, 5, 8, 18, 27, 32, 36, 39, 40, 49, 58, 61, 63, 68, 72, 74, 81, 83, "True" or if you answered questions, 1, 2, 3, 4, 6, 10, 16, 17, 21, 23, 24, 29, 46, 47, 54, 57, 69, "False" there may be some room for improvement in this area.

If you feel your self-esteem could stand to be improved, there are many good books in the "Self-Help" section of any bookstore,[3] or you may want to check at your local library for books on the subject.

If merely reading books doesn't do the trick, you may need professional help. In seeking professional help, be sure the professional you choose is qualified and is someone with whom you feel comfortable.[4]

Self-confidence goes hand in hand with a healthy self-esteem. Usually when someone suffers from a low self-esteem, she also is lacking in self-confidence. One way to build self-confidence is to focus on your strengths instead of your weakness. In fact, right now, I want you to get a piece of paper and a pen or pencil. Write down at least ten things about yourself you consider to be your strengths. Please write down as many things as you can think of, but at least write down ten things that are your strengths. If you have trouble thinking of ten strengths, then this is definitely an area where you could use some improvement. [5]

Being secure in yourself is another important factor in being a whole person. If you are fraught with insecurities, then it will be difficult for you to feel secure in a relationship with a man. This is one area where many women allow themselves to be deceived. It is so easy to think, "If I just have a man in my life, then I will feel secure." This is a false expectation. It is important to feel secure in yourself *before* you enter into a relationship with a man. If you are expecting a man to *make* you feel secure, you are setting yourself up for disappointment. This is not to say that you shouldn't expect to feel secure in a relationship with a man. What I am saying is that it is not anyone else's responsibility to *make* you feel secure. It is up to you to work out your own sense of security. This means not allowing the actions or words of others to cause you to feel insecure. Feelings of insecurity are very closely tied to feelings of inadequacy. So, if you feel inadequate in any way at all, then this may be an area for you to work on improving.[5]

EMOTIONAL AND MENTAL HEALTH

Emotional and mental health are crucial if you expect to establish a satisfying long-term relationship with a man. Here again, don't succumb to the "fairy tale" notion that your "Handsome Prince" is going to "rescue" you from your emotional problems. If you have emotional problems, then do whatever it takes to work them out yourself. The less emotional "baggage" you bring to a relationship, the better your chance for a happy relationship. (At this point, we won't go into the emotional "baggage" he may have. That will be discussed in a later chapter. Right now, we are focusing on you.)

No matter what emotional scars you may be carrying around from your past, you and only you are responsible for taking the steps necessary to deal with those issues to become as emotionally healthy as it is possible for you to be.

Very closely related to emotional health is mental health. This is a rather deep subject, and I am neither qualified nor inclined to determine the state of your mental health. However, if you answered questions, 7, 11, 13, 15, 19, 22, 28, 30, 33, 34, 38, 42, 43, 50, 52, 60, 78, "True" or if you answered questions, 12, 14, 20, 35, 37, 51, 56, 62, 64, 65, 67, 70, 73, 75, 77, 80, 82, "False," this may be an indication that it would be wise to get some help to work out any of the emotional or mental health issues you may have. It is your responsibility to discover where you are as far as mental health goes, and if you see room for improvement, then take the necessary steps. If you feel you need professional help, then seek out someone who is qualified and you feel can help you.[6]

Chapter 3

Take Care Of Yourself

Self-respect is one of the ingredients necessary in taking care of yourself. If you don't respect yourself, then it follows you won't take very good care of yourself. If you won't take good care of yourself, then it is unrealistic to think anyone else is going to take care of you. You may in all likelihood find *someone* who is willing to take on the task of taking care of you when you won't take care of yourself, but I can assure you, it won't be a happy, healthy relationship that is built on a solid foundation.

So, what is involved in taking good care of yourself? The following are a few of the things that fall into this category:

Eat a balanced diet. This can sometimes be a challenge since commercials push a host of products on us that leave a lot to be desired as far as nutrition is concerned. Also, many of us lead frantic, rushed lives and eat far too often at "fast food" restaurants. As far as I am concerned, the average American diet does not provide proper nutrition to maintain a strong healthy body. What I mean by "average American diet" is as follows: a diet high in processed, refined foods (for example; refined white flour, refined white sugar, convenience foods, mixes, foods high in additives and artificial ingredients), a diet high in meat protein, starches and caffeine and low in fresh fruits and vegetables. Also, the average American eats way too many foods cooked or reheated in a microwave oven.[7]

Here is a rule of thumb that you may find helpful. As much as possible, eat whole, natural foods. If you have the opportunity to purchase "home-grown" produce from a farmer's market or co-op, do so. Not only does "home-grown" produce taste better, but also it is generally better for you. Whenever you can, avoid highly refined, processed foods. Below is a chart to use as a guideline.

Foods with a high nutritional content

Fresh fruits
Fresh vegetables
Fresh eggs
Tofu
Soy products
Dairy products[8]
Lean meats
Whole grains, such as: whole wheat, corn, brown rice, barley, old-fashioned rolled oats, etc.
Nuts and seeds, such as: walnuts, pecans, almonds, pine nuts, pistachios, cashews, poppy seeds, sesame seeds, sunflower seeds, etc.
Sprouts, such as: bean sprouts, alfalfa sprouts, radish sprouts, sunflower sprouts, etc.
Dried beans, such as: navy beans, kidney beans, pinto beans, red beans, black beans, lima beans, butter beans, green peas, yellow peas, garbanzo beans, soybeans, lentils, etc.
Natural vegetable oils, such as: olive oil, sunflower oil, avocado oil, safflower oil, sesame oil, soy oil, etc.
Natural sweeteners, such as: real maple syrup, molasses, date sugar, raw, unprocessed honey
Potatoes, sweet potatoes, yams
Apple cider vinegar

Herbs, such as: basil, bay leaves, oregano, paprika, dill seed, dill weed, mustard seed, celery seed, savory, onion, garlic, fennel, marjoram, parsley, sage, rosemary, and thyme, etc.

Spices, such as: cayenne pepper, cumin, ginger, cloves, allspice, nutmeg, cinnamon, paprika, curry powder, etc.

Foods to avoid

Deep fried foods
Fatty foods
Carbonated beverages
Iceberg or head lettuce
Foods cooked or reheated in a microwave oven[7]

Start reading the list of ingredients in the foods you normally buy and avoid foods containing *any* of the following: white flour, white sugar, sucrose, dextrose, artificial ingredients, canola oil, hydrogenated vegetable oil, corn syrup, high fructose corn syrup, fructose, lard, enriched flour, chemicals, monosodium glutamate, any kind of hydrolyzed protein, cottonseed oil, palm oil.

If you want to learn more about proper nutrition, there are many books on this subject.[9]

Another way you can take care of yourself is to be as close to your ideal weight as possible. There are four good reasons for this:

1) You will look better.
2) You will feel better, physically.
3) You will feel better about yourself.
4) You will increase your chances to live a longer and healthier life.

This is not a "diet" or "weight loss" book, so I won't go into a long dissertation on this subject. There are many reasons a person could be overweight. Very few of those reasons are "beyond a person's control." Many of the reasons are associated very closely with self-esteem and self-worth. The bottom line is if you are more than 15 lbs. over your ideal weight, you may want to determine the cause and do something about it. For whatever it is worth, it has been my observation that most "diet plans" don't work because they are temporary. You can lose weight by "going on a diet" but as soon as you go back to the way you were eating before, the pounds come right back on. Permanent weight loss requires a permanent change in the way you eat, in the way you think, in the way you feel about yourself and a permanent change in your activity level.[10]

Another issue I feel needs to be addressed here is being underweight. This can be just a much a threat to your health and well-being as being overweight. If you are so thin that your bones are prominent, it may be a good idea to talk to a doctor or other professional who can offer sound advice to help you gain weight.[11]

Adequate exercise is also a necessary component to taking care of

> Being underweight . . . can be just as much a threat to your health as being overweight.

yourself. This can sometimes be a challenge if you drive to work every day and sit at a desk. You don't have to spend a lot of money to join a health club in order to get the proper exercise. There are lots of things you can do to get the exercise you need. Dancing, sports (volleyball, tennis, racquet ball, Frisbee, softball, ping-pong, etc.), walking, bicycling, swimming, etc. Pretty much anything that will get your body active and your heart rate up. I would not recommend that you buy any of those "handy" exercise machines you see advertised on TV. Most people use those for a short time and then sell them in the newspaper or at a garage sale.

Don't pay a lot of money . . .

Wow! What a deal!	First Month
Second Month	Six Months Later

For something you will hardly use.

You are more likely to be consistent with your exercise if it is something you truly enjoy. It is just human nature to prefer to do something that is fun rather than something that is work.

Of course, if you really want to join a health club, that is certainly an option. I will caution you, however. Again, most people go for a while and then get too busy to go and drop out. The health clubs know this and that is why they can always oversell memberships. If you are going to join, do whatever it takes to keep yourself going and get the most out of your membership.

The next subject in taking care of yourself I would like to address is personal hygiene. Part of respecting yourself is making sure you keep yourself clean. This means regular showers or baths, brushing *and* flossing your teeth two or three times a day, and brushing or combing your hair *at least* once a day.

It is also advisable to use something to minimize body odor. When you are on your menstrual period, it is important to change your feminine protection often.

In our society, personal hygiene products are pushed at us from every direction. Most people get the message that personal hygiene is important, but unfortunately, some do not. If you neglect your personal hygiene, chances are, most men won't want to be near you. The exception might be a man who practices poor personal hygiene himself.

It is important, however, not to go overboard in your attempt to keep your body clean. Too much of a good thing can even be harmful. Your body secretes natural oil that lubricates and helps to protect your skin. If you bathe too much, your skin can dry out or even start itching, cracking or peeling.

I'll give you an example. When I was in my twenties, I lived in a dry, desert climate. I was taking one or two baths every day and using a harsh, deodorant soap. My skin dried out so much that I started itching all over. The itching got so bad, I couldn't even sleep at night. I went to a dermatologist to find out why my skin was itching so badly. After asking me a lot of questions, he told me to stop using deodorant soap and start using a "super-fatted" soap of some kind. He also told me to stop taking full baths every day and to instead take "sponge" baths more often and only take full baths 3 or 4 times a week.

So, you have to take a lot of things into account when deciding how often you need to bathe. If you live in a humid climate, you can probably bathe more often than if you live in a dry climate. You also need to consider your skin type; does it tend to be more oily or more dry? The answer to this question also needs to be considered in your determination of how often to bathe. Also, if you have dry skin, it is best to not use a harsh, deodorant soap that will dry it out more. Bottom line, use good judgment and common sense. Keep yourself clean without "scrubbing yourself to death."

Keep yourself clean . .

without scrubbing yourself to death!

There is another thing I would like to mention while on this subject. There are many personal hygiene products sold

that may not be good for you. Body powder and feminine hygiene spray, for instance.[12] Just because it is advertised on TV or in your favorite magazine doesn't mean it is good for you. Be sensible and do a little research yourself. Generally speaking, the more natural any product is, the better the chances it will not be harmful. Keep in mind, though, that even some natural ingredients can be harmful, i.e., "talc."
[12] Avoid as much as possible products that contain a lot of chemicals that you can't pronounce or don't know what they are. You don't need to be a "victim" of advertising and feel that you have to go out and buy every product you see promoted. Take personal responsibility for the personal products you purchase and buy only the ones you know will be good for you.

Related to personal hygiene is making yourself as attractive as possible. It is your choice whether to wear makeup or not. Many women are happy to "go natural" and not wear any makeup at all. If you don't wear makeup, my suggestion is to use some kind of skin care products to keep your face clean and moisturized. The older you get, the more important this is, as aging tends to dry out your skin.

If you do wear makeup, *don't overdo it!!!!* Makeup so thick it looks like it was applied with a trowel, is *not* attractive. You may want to consult with a beauty consultant if you have questions on this subject. It is also a good idea to find out what makeup colors work best for you. [13] Not everyone can wear the same colors successfully. The idea is to wear makeup in such a way as to enhance your natural beauty. If someone sees you and he or she thinks, "What a beautiful woman!" then you have your makeup on right. On the other hand, if they think, "Woooh, look at the *makeup* on that woman!" you may want to change how you do your makeup.[13]

Since you can't possibly know what other people are thinking, you will have to be honest with yourself and perhaps enlist the help of a friend or acquaintance who is willing to be honest with you. Don't wear your feelings on your sleeve here. The point is to find out if your makeup enhances your natural beauty or detracts from it. If you don't know, you can't do anything to improve it.

Even if you usually wear makeup, there are some times when it may be better not to. For instance, a male friend of mine once told me about a date he had. He took this girl to the beach on a hot day and said he watched her face literally "melt" in the sun. He did not think it was attractive. Personally, I have found that when I vacation in an extremely humid climate, it is better to "nix" the liquid or crème foundation, since it keeps "running" on your face and looks awful!

As an aside, and related to makeup, I would like to say a brief word about perfume or cologne. The right fragrance can enhance your attractiveness; however, no matter how pleasant the fragrance of a perfume or cologne, overdoing it can be a big turn off to most men. Use fragrance sparingly. A short time after you put on a fragrance, you become desensitized to it and may think that you need to apply more. Just because you can no longer detect it does not mean that it has worn off. Other people will be able to tell you have a fragrance on. Subtle is better. If someone can tell you have a fragrance on from ten feet away, you have too much on.

Let's talk about hair. Find out what hairstyle flatters your face the most. Again, there are professionals that you can consult to give you some pointers. If you don't want to go to a professional, then find books that illustrate face shapes and appropriate hairstyles that go with each shape.

The color of your clothing is also important to being attractive. For years, I wore all the wrong colors for me, because I didn't know any better. I just picked colors I liked and didn't even consider if they looked good on me or not.

There are professionals who study color and can help you determine what colors are best for you. Colors are divided into the four seasons: spring, summer, autumn, and winter. Have a professional determine which you are and find out the colors that go with that "season" and start wearing those colors. [14] You will be amazed at the difference it makes. You will start getting compliments more often, because wearing the right colors for you will make you glow!

The last subject I would like to cover on taking care of yourself is being neat and clean. When you go out in public, don't just "throw" yourself together. I don't mean you have to get all dressed up every time you go out of the house. What I mean is, whatever you wear, make sure you look neat and clean. Don't wear wrinkled or dirty clothes. If you are wearing hose, take an extra pair with you, just in case you get a run in the pair you are wearing. The next thing I am going to say may not apply to you, but there are some to whom it may apply. Do not *ever* go out in public with curlers or rollers in your hair!

Right along with personal neatness, I recommend that you learn how to keep your living quarters neat and clean as well. I don't mean you have to be some kind of "Suzie Homemaker" or that where you live has to look like *House and Garden.* Just do your best to keep the trash picked up and thrown away and avoid having clutter all over the place. I grew up in a house that had so much clutter that you had to clear off a space to have somewhere to sit down. There was not one "flat surface" in the house that was ever kept cleared off.

Don't be a slob. Pick up after yourself and put things away. If you don't have a place to put everything away, then either you live in too small a place, or you have too much stuff, or a combination of both. Get rid of everything that you really don't need. Don't be a "pack rat." I don't want to hear "that's just the way I am" either. No one is born a slob or a pack rat. Those are habits that are learned and can be unlearned as well. If you didn't learn how to keep house from your mother (I certainly didn't learn from mine), then do whatever it takes to learn a few housekeeping skills from somewhere else. The only man who will enjoy living with a slob or pack rat is another slob or pack rat. If you really *want* to live in a dump, then you can ignore the last two paragraphs.

Chapter 4

A Better You

I am going to assume that most of you reading this book are *not* perfect people. That being the case, it is advisable to have a program for improving yourself.

There are many good books that can help you to do this.[15] You may be able to find some or all of these books at the library so you don't have to go out and buy them all. Another suggestion is if you have a girlfriend who is also interested in self-improvement, you can share books.

There are also some really good audiotape series and videotape series on the subject of self-improvement.[16] One word of caution... there are some series out there on this subject that are very expensive. Don't get sucked into thinking that just because it costs a lot of money, it is something really valuable. Get referrals or recommendations from people who have been through that series and ask them if they think it was worth what they paid for it.

There is one self-improvement seminar that I personally recommend highly. It is the "Dale Carnegie Course." This course does cost quite a lot, but it is well worth it. I took the "Dale Carnegie Course" when I was in my early twenties. It was a positive turning point in my life.[17]

After I graduated from the course I was a volunteer "graduate assistant" in three different classes. It was always a joy to me to see how much people improved over the 14 weeks of the course. I personally don't know anyone who has gone through the course who hasn't received a positive benefit from it.

There are many other ways in which you can improve yourself. The possibilities are only limited by your imagination. Here are a few examples to get you thinking along those lines. Learn a new skill; Take a class; Learn a foreign language; Take up a new sport; Get more education; Take music lessons; Read some good books; Take martial arts; etc., etc., etc.

Another way to improve yourself is to learn how to give to others in a positive, healthy way. I say it this way because some women think they have to give everything of themselves to others and can never say "no" when someone asks them to give of themselves. That is *not* what I am talking about here. Healthy life is a balance. If you have learned how to love yourself properly as is discussed earlier in this book, then you will know what I am talking about.

The kind of giving I am talking about is giving of your time and your talents to help those in the community in which you live. There are many worthy causes that would welcome volunteer workers. [18] Look for ways you can do something for others and not get paid for it. You will be amazed at how giving will bless your life and make you a better person.

It is my philosophy that you are never too old to learn something new and you are never so "good" a person that you couldn't stand some improving. Always look for ways to improve yourself and make yourself a better person.

CULTIVATE A POSITIVE MENTAL ATTITUDE

Developing a positive mental attitude was a challenge for me as it may be for some of you. I was a pessimist all the way through high school and into my early twenties. Thankfully, I had a very good friend that was honest with me about how others saw me. People were avoiding me because when they asked me how I was, I told them and it was always bad. My life was one sad story after another and after a while, people just didn't want to hear it. Now that I know better, I don't blame them.

It is important for you to understand that while you can't always control what happens to you, you can choose how you will react to it. You can react negatively or positively. If you are a pessimist, I urge you to work on cultivating a positive mental attitude. Not only will you feel better about yourself, but also others will enjoy being around you more. No one likes being around someone who gripes and complains about everything all the time.

You may be asking yourself, "How do I change from a negative attitude to a positive attitude?" Well, I can tell you from my experience, it probably won't happen overnight. Chances are that if you have a negative attitude, it took some time to get that way, and it will take some time to change.

You may want to start by reading some books on positive mental attitude.[19] Also, there are some excellent scriptures that will help you to focus your mind on positive things.[20]

Positive affirmations are also a good way to cultivate a positive mental attitude. There are books that suggest positive affirmations[21] or you can make your own. If you don't have a clue what I am talking about when I say "positive affirmation," let me explain. A positive affirmation is a positive statement that you want to be true in your life and about you whether or not you believe it is true right now. I have heard it said, "What you think about, you bring about."[22] Since I have found this statement to be true, one way to change your outlook on life is to change what you think. You can help to change what you think by using positive affirmations. One of my favorite ways to write my own positive affirmations is to pick scriptures and personalize them.[23]

If you have never used positive affirmations before, please understand that when you first start, you will probably have a little voice in your head saying, "Those things aren't true about you or about your life." Ignore it! In time it will fade and after that, it will disappear altogether. You need to be persistent in order to effectively change your attitude from negative to positive. For some reason I have not come to fully understand myself yet, it seems as though those things in life worth having require some effort on our part. Cultivating a positive mental attitude is no different. Please trust me on this; it will be worth the effort. Just think of it this way. Do you want to be remembered as someone who has a dark cloud hanging over her head all the time? Or would you rather be remembered as someone who is happy and cheerful all the time, and the kind of person who brings sunshine into the room when she walks in?

Your persistence will pay off and after being consistent in reading your positive affirmations daily (I recommend you read them out loud whenever possible) you will start to notice that more and more, the things you are saying in your positive affirmations are true about you.

There are also some health benefits to cultivating a positive mental attitude. There are many studies that have been done that show beyond a shadow of a doubt that those with a positive attitude are healthier and sick less often than those with a negative attitude. [24] I am convinced that those with a positive attitude not only live longer, but they also have happier lives.

KNOW WHAT YOU WANT OUT OF LIFE

If you want to find the man with whom you will share the rest of your life, it is important for you to know what you want out of life. It stands to reason that if you have no idea what you want, then how will you know when you get it?

Here are some questions for you to ask yourself. When you have the answers, it is important to write them down! Be as specific as you can be.

1) What do I want to do with my life?
2) Do I want to have a career, if so what career do I want?
3) If I don't choose a career, what kind of work do I want to do?
4) What state do I want to live in?
5) What country (nation) do I want to live in?
6) Do I want to live in the city, the suburbs, or the country?
7) Do I want to live close to work, or do I want to commute?
8) What do I want to contribute to the community in which I live?
9) How close do I want to be to my family (mother, father, brothers and sisters)?
10) How much education do I want?
11) What is my purpose in life?
12) Do I plan to marry?
13) Do I plan to have children?
14) How do I want people to remember me?

I realize that some of these questions are pretty "heavy" and not easy to answer. You don't have to come up with the "perfect" answer to each question. I only pose them so you will have something to think about and a place to start. You may think of other questions as well. If so, then answer them also. If you ask yourself these same questions at different times in your life, you will probably come up with different answers. That's okay. You have the right to change your mind as your life unfolds. Don't let the fact that your expectations will change discourage you from answering the questions for yourself right now. It is important for you to have goals and objectives to work toward. Even though those goals and objectives may change over time, it is always advisable to have something in front of you that you are working towards. Think of it as a journey *not* a destination. Don't worry about any obstacles that might get in your way as you are working toward your goals. As Henry Ford said, "Obstacles are those frightful things you see when you take your eyes off your goal."

Living your life without some kind of idea of what you expect out of life is like being in a boat adrift on the ocean without a sail or motor or oars. You have no idea where you will end up. Don't trust your future to chance and happenstance. Have an idea of what you want and where you are going in your life. Also, be sure your goals are *your* goals and *not* the goals your parents, teachers or friends have for you. Be your own person. More on this later.

KNOW YOUR PRIORITIES

What are your priorities? Before you establish a long-term relationship with a man, it is important you know what are the most important things to you. We can get so caught up in the "whirlwind" of life that we sometimes forget or neglect what is really important to us. One way I have heard this put is, "When you are up to your neck in alligators, it is difficult to remember that your main objective was to drain the swamp!"[25]

Perhaps the best way to not let life "get in the way" is to clearly know what your priorities are and write them down and keep them close at hand to help you remember what is important to you.

For those of you who are still unclear what I mean when I say "priorities," I mean making a list of all the things that are important to you and putting them in the order of importance with the most important thing first.

As a simple exercise and to give you a better idea of what we are talking about here, the following is a list of things that many people consider important. This is *not* a comprehensive list. It is only an example. Arrange the following list in the order of importance to you with the most important thing first, the second most important thing next, and so on to the least important thing. Keep in mind that some of your priorities may change over time as your life changes.

Education	Church	Self
Work	God	Health
Family	Physical Fitness	Recreation
Entertainment	Community	Politics

Once you have determined what the most important thing to you is, do your best to keep that number one in your life. I have heard it said, "The main thing is to keep the main thing the main thing." [26] Try your best not to lose your focus on what is important to you. Knowing your priorities will help you later to determine if the man you are considering as a lifemate is compatible with you.

BE ASSERTIVE

Assertiveness is something that many women in our society find challenging. Oftentimes, women are taught to be "nice," which implies always being compliant to the wishes of others even when their wishes are unreasonable. Assertive does *not* mean being pushy or always insisting on having your own way. That is just plain rude.

What I mean by "assertive" is standing your ground and not letting others push you around when you know in your heart that you are right.

> Assertive does not mean being pushy . . . or always insisting on having your own way!

There is a balance here and you have to exercise good judgment to know when to stand up for yourself and when to give in.

Let me give you some examples. When you go to a car dealer and know exactly what kind of car you want to buy, don't let the salesperson talk you into buying something else. If you get a bill in the mail that you know is wrong; don't just pay it, get on the phone and talk to someone to get it corrected. If you are at the deli and someone comes in after you and tries to get served first, say, "Excuse me, but I believe I was here first."

On the other hand, there are some times when you can be right and it is better to give in for a number of reasons. Some of the reasons to give in might be to save a relationship, to save a life, or to save your self a lot of heartache and grief. Here are some examples. If your best friend wants to go shopping and you really want to go to a movie, it may be better to give in and go shopping rather than insist on going to a movie at the risk of straining the relationship. Being assertive behind the wheel of a car can be dangerous. There are a lot of wackos out there. This is *not* the best place to be assertive. With the high incidence of "road rage," "getting into it" with another motorist could cost you your life. As to an example of someone causing themselves undue heartache and grief over standing up for what was right, I suggest you rent the movie, *The Jack Bull*.[27] The main character was standing up for noble principles, but he didn't know when to quit and give in, and it cost him dearly. Only you can determine when to stand up for yourself and when to give in.

If this is an area where you need help, there are books that deal with this issue in depth.[28] There are also assertiveness training classes if you think you would benefit from something along those lines.[29]

LISTEN AND BE THOUGHTFUL AND CONSIDERATE OF OTHERS

Listening is a skill that you would be wise to learn and practice. I can't tell you how many times I have heard, "God gave you two ears and one mouth, so you should listen twice as much as you talk." [30] Perhaps you have heard this as well. There is another quote that comes to mind here as well, "Knowledge speaks, but wisdom listens." [31]

I must confess, this has been a real challenge for me as it may be for some of you. I really love to talk and always think that what I have to say is *so* important. What I have learned, however is that when I keep quiet and let others do the talking, I get to know them better and I sometimes even learn something.

If listening is something that you find difficult to do, try asking the other person questions to get him or her to talk. There are many times this has worked for me. Also, you might try what is called "reflective listening" which is saying back to the person what he or she has said to you (only in different words) so he or she knows that you really did hear what he or she said.

Listening to others is just one way you show thoughtfulness and consideration. There are many other ways to do this as well. It is important to treat others as we would like to be treated. I am sure you have heard of the "Golden Rule," "Do unto others as you would have them do unto you." [32] Well, that is good advice. However, I do want to expand on this.

Practicing the "Golden Rule" exactly to the letter does not always work. Let me explain. One time I was living in a fourplex and all four families shared the laundry facilities. I washed a load of clothes and when I went to put them into the dryer, someone else's clothes were in the dryer. Thinking about what I would want my neighbor to do for me, I folded the clothes and put them on top of the dryer. My neighbor was furious with me. She had this "thing" about other people touching her clothes and was really upset that I had folded her clothes and put them on the dryer. So, even though I acted out of what I would have wanted someone to do for me, in this case it was not the right thing to do. My point is you have to go beyond just doing what you would want others to do for you, and be thoughtful and considerate enough to do for others what *they* would want you to do. Of course, sometimes it is impossible for you to know what others might want. However, instead of just assuming that someone else would want to be treated the same way you would, do your best to find out how others want to be treated and treat them that way.

You can't rely on our culture to teach you how to be thoughtful and considerate of others. The media pushes a multitude of ideas that are egocentric and self-serving. The phrase "what's in it for me" is commonplace.

The best place I know to find out how to be mindful of others is the Bible.[33] You may be saying to yourself, "Here we go again. She's going to preach to us!" Well, that may be your perception, but it is certainly not my intention. Whether you "believe in" the Bible or not, it contains wisdom that has stood the test of time and is just as valid as when it was written, centuries and sometimes even thousands of years ago. Our technology may change, but the essential nature of people remains the same.

One of the ways you can be thoughtful and considerate of others is to always do your best in whatever you do. In other words, don't *ever* be conned into thinking that doing things halfway is "good enough." I am reminded of a couple of sayings that you may have heard, "A job worth doing is a job worth doing well,"[34] and "If you don't have time to do it right, when will you have time to do it over?"[34]

In our society marginal performance is commonplace. I challenge you to raise your standards above this and always do the best you can at whatever you do. If you give 100% to every task you do, you can have peace in knowing that you gave your best. You will be surprised at the personal satisfaction you will receive by doing this one thing.

STAND FOR AND BELIEVE IN SOMETHING

My mother used to say to me, "Those who stand for nothing, fall for anything."[35] Well, my mom wasn't right about a lot of things, but she *was* right about that.

It is important that you stand for something. You can decide what that "something" is. Whatever it is, it is important that it be bigger than you. If all you stand for is you, there is no room in your life for anyone else.

It is also important that you not be "wishy washy" or a chameleon. What I mean by "wishy washy" is not having any idea what you stand for or what is important to you. One day you're this way the next day you're that way. You change with the wind so you never really make a firm stand for anything at all.

What I mean by being a chameleon is, changing what you stand for to "blend in" with those around you at the time. Just as a chameleon changes color to blend in with its surroundings, you change what you stand for so you blend in with others. You want so much to be accepted by others that you say you stand for whatever those around you stand for, whether you really feel that way or not. When you are with your parents, you stand for what they stand for. When you are with your friends, you stand for what they stand for, even though it is different from what your parents stand for. When you are with one date, you tell him that you stand for the same things he does, and as your dates change, what you stand for changes accordingly. This is a sign of insecurity and a failure to trust your own judgment. If this sounds like you, then this is an area where you could use some improvement. Please refer back to Chapter 2 on trusting your own judgment and being secure in yourself and work on this.

Along with standing for something is believing in something. You may or may not believe in God. It is not my place to tell you what you should or should not believe in. You have been given freedom of choice on this matter. I can however make a strong case for belief in God.

It is well documented that those who have a belief in God have many advantages over those who have no belief in God. According to many psychological studies that have been done regarding the effect a belief in God has on serious illness and the healing of the body, the studies show time and again that those with a belief in God fare much better than those who have no belief in God.[36]

Belief in God and belief in a life after death offers a great hope and comfort that those without such a belief do not have. Knowing that there is a God in Heaven who loves you and cares about what happens to you, helps you to deal with adversity in your life much more effectively than believing there is no God.

I can tell you from personal experience that if I did not believe that there is a loving God who cares about me, in all likelihood, I would not be here today, for I would have taken my life long ago. Though I cannot prove to you beyond a shadow of a doubt that there is a loving God who cares for me, my believing so has helped me to get through the dark times of my life and has kept me alive and hopeful. For that reason alone, my belief in God has value.

Belief that there is a life after death and that in Heaven you will be reunited with those you love who have died, offers great comfort to those who have lost loved ones in death. If I may, I would like to share a personal example here. My first child was a girl. Her name was Rachel. She was born with a chromosome defect and died in my arms (at the hospital) when she was two weeks old. I believe she is with

God in Heaven and that when I die, I will see her again. It would be impossible for me to prove this, but believing it gives me great comfort and hope, and for that reason alone, it has value.

Belief in God and belief in the Bible helps one to have a code to live by. Those who practice what the Bible teaches are happy, healthy (physically, emotionally, mentally and spiritually), better neighbors, compassionate, loving and kind.

Some of you at this point may be saying to yourself, "I know people who say they believe in God or who say they are 'Christians' and they are not nice people at all." Well, I would like to quote what Jesus says about this, "Not everyone who says to me, 'Lord, Lord,' will enter the kingdom of heaven, but only he [or she] who does the will of my Father who is in heaven." (Matt. 7:21).[37]

What I said was those who "practice" what the Bible teaches. There are many who profess a belief in God or who say they are "Christians" who do *not* at all practice what the Bible teaches. They only give it "lip service." I am not talking about them. I am talking about those who have an intimate relationship with the Creator of the Universe and with His Son, Jesus Christ, and who are guided by the Holy Spirit dwelling within them. I am talking about those who diligently *study* the Bible on a regular basis and strive to put it into practice in their lives.

I am not a Christian because that is what I was taught to believe. I am a Christian because I have studied all of the major world religions and have come to the conclusion that Christianity is the *only* faith that holds up under close scrutiny and examination. All of the rest failed that test.

I find it quite interesting that I am not the only one who has come to this conclusion. There are many stories of atheists who have sought to disprove the Bible and in the process of trying to do so, have become Christians. There are also those who have come from non-religious backgrounds that have become Christians as a result of conducting a critical study of the world's major religions.

Here are some examples: C.S. Lewis[38] was a professor at Oxford University in England. He was an atheist and sought to disprove the Bible. Not only could he not disprove the Bible, but he became a Christian in the process. He then went on to write many books on the subject of Christianity. He wrote *The Chronicles of Narnia, The Screwtape Letters, The Problem of Pain,* and *Mere Christianity* to name a few. I recommend all of his books.[39]

Richard Wurmbrand[40] grew up in Romania and was heavily influenced by Communism. In his youth, he did not believe in God. After taking a closer look at the Bible, he became a Christian, even though to do so was against the law. He spent many years in prison and was tortured for his faith. Pastor Wurmbrand has written many books about his experiences.[41]

John Clayton[42] is a scientist who was an atheist until he undertook a critical study of the Bible. He read the Bible through from cover to cover four times during his sophomore year in college for the explicit purpose of finding scientific contradictions in it and was simply not able to find any. Subsequently, John Clayton became a Christian. He now devotes much of his time to providing thinking, seeking people with scientific evidence that God does exist and that the Bible is His Word.

Dr. Hugh Ross[43] came from a non-religious background. In his search for the truth he read all of the holy books of the major world religions. The only one of these holy books he found to be error free was the Bible. Dr. Ross became a Christian and has written many books on the subject of science and the Bible.[44] In 1986, Dr. Ross founded "Reasons to Believe."

I challenge you to do your own research and study. Don't believe in something simply because that is what you were taught, or that is what your parents or your friends believe.

Do your "homework" and check things out for yourself. This may take some time, but it will be worth it. Belief built on the solid foundation of your own research and study will become unshakable and help you to stand strong through the storms of life.

PRACTICE SELF-CONTROL AND ACCEPT PERSONAL RESPONSIBILITY

I have noticed over the last several years that in our society we have become more and more lax in the area of self-control. Discipline of any kind seems to be a thing of the past. There are actually psychologists who promote the idea of allowing children to do whatever they want to do. These same psychologists teach parents to never impose any kind of boundaries on children and to allow them to grow up "free" and unrestricted. Perhaps it is because of this prevailing permissive attitude in our society that it has become difficult for so many adults to practice self-control.

Be that as it may, self-control is still an important quality to possess if one expects to be the best person she can be. It is even more important to practice self-control in our relationships with others.

So, you may be asking yourself, "What exactly is self-control and how do I learn self-control if it wasn't taught to me?" First of all, self-control is just that, controlling your self. This means *not* acting out everything that goes through your head. For example, someone may make you so angry you feel like causing him/her physical harm. Self-control is not acting on those feelings. Self-control is evaluating everything you feel like doing *before* you act and making the determination if that action is appropriate or not. If what you feel like doing is not appropriate to the situation then don't do it. That is self-control.

Perhaps you were not taught to practice self-control. If so, be encouraged. Self-control is something that is never too late to learn. A method I have found helpful in developing self-control is whenever I have an impulse to do something, rather than acting on it immediately, I imagine the outcome and consequences of that action and then decide if the outcome and consequences are negative or positive. If the results of that action would be negative, then I don't act on that impulse. If the results of that action would be positive, then I follow through with the action. Stopping to think about the consequences of what you do before you do it can save you a lot of grief and heartache. Many of the difficulties I have experienced in my life could have been avoided if I had practiced self-control and resisted the temptation to act impulsively on my feelings.

Self-control also means controlling your tongue. Not controlling one's tongue is such a common problem, we have sayings about it, such as, "loose lips sink ships," "open mouth, insert foot," "a closed mouth gathers no feet," "foot in mouth disease," "diarrhea of the mouth," and "I'm talking and I can't shut up!" We refer to someone who doesn't control his/her tongue as having a "sharp" tongue. Children defend themselves against other children with sharp tongues by saying the following: "sticks and stones can break my bones, but names can never hurt me" or "I'm rubber and you're glue. Everything you say bounces off of me and sticks to you." The Bible also has a great deal to say about controlling one's tongue.[45]

The best story I can think of that illustrates why it is important to control one's tongue is the following:

There was a young woman who was in the habit of saying hurtful things to people when she became angry. One day her supervisor took her to the twentieth floor of the office building where they worked. The supervisor walked the young woman over to the window, opened it and gave her a feather pillow with the end cut open. The supervisor then asked the young woman to dump the feathers (from the pillow) out the window. As the feathers blew out the window, the supervisor told the young woman that the feathers represented all of the unkind words she had said in anger. The supervisor then told the young woman to go out into the city and gather up all the feathers and put them back in the pillow. "But, that would be impossible!" protested the young woman. The supervisor replied, "Just as it is impossible to take back hurtful words said in anger."[46] The young woman got the point. I hope you do as well.

I am also reminded of a story that illustrates not only the importance of controlling one's tongue, but also the importance of controlling one's temper:

There once was a little boy who had a bad temper. His Father gave him a bag of nails and told him that every time he lost his temper, he must hammer a nail into the back of the fence. The first day the boy had driven thirty-seven nails into the fence.

Over the next few weeks, as he learned to control his anger, the number of nails hammered daily gradually dwindled down. He discovered it was easier to hold his temper than to drive those nails into the fence.

Finally the day came when the boy didn't lose his temper at all. He told his father about it and the father suggested that the boy now pull out one nail for each day that he was able to hold his temper.

The days passed and the young boy was finally able to tell his father that all the nails were gone. The father took his son by the hand and led him to the fence. He said, "You have done well, my son, but look at the holes in the fence. The fence will never be the same. When you say things in anger, they leave a scar just like this one. You can put a knife in a man and draw it out. It won't matter how many times you say I'm sorry, the wound is still there. A verbal wound is as bad as a physical one." The little boy learned a valuable lesson that day.[46] I hope you find value in this story.

Closely related to self-control is accepting personal responsibility. Our society does not any longer teach people to be responsible for their lives and their actions. We live in a society where it is always someone else's "fault." We have lawyers who make their living by convincing people to sue someone else for their own stupid mistakes. Some psychologists and psychiatrists make their living by convincing people that someone else (usually from one's childhood) is to blame for all the problems in their lives. For those of you who think that someone else is to blame for everything that is wrong in your life, I recommend you listen to the song "Get Over It!" by the Eagles.[47]

You, and only you are responsible for who you are and where you are in your life. When you became an adult, you became responsible for your own life. Who and what you are is your choice. It is not your mother's or father's fault or your brothers' or sisters' fault. It is not your aunt's, uncle's or cousin's fault. It's not your teachers' fault, your coach's fault or your pastor's, preacher's, priest's, or nun's fault. Did I leave anyone out? Well, it's not that person's fault either! You are the person you are and you are where you are in your life because of your own choices and decisions. You are responsible for your life and your actions. No matter what anyone else tells you, there is no one else to blame. If you want someone to blame, look in the mirror!

You are where you are in your life as a result of all of your own best decisions. Until you come face to face with the truth that you decide what kind of person you are and you decide what your life is, you cannot make any real progress in your life. As long as you go through life blaming others for your life, you will remain "stuck" in the "twilight zone" of denial. If it is a challenge for you to accept personal responsibility, there are many good books on the subject.[48]

BE KIND AND LOVING

Your behavior towards others says a lot about you as a person. Learn to cultivate kind and loving behavior towards those with whom you come in contact. For most of us, it is easy to be kind and loving towards people who are nice to us and we care about. It is more difficult to be kind and loving towards those we don't like or those who are unkind to us.

I have had lots of personal experience with this one. I used to think that if I was ugly to a sales clerk or customer service representative about a situation that made me angry, it didn't matter because that person wasn't a part of my life. I was "famous" for giving someone "a piece of my mind" whenever something happened that upset me. I would say mean, cutting things to salesclerks, secretaries, managers, and customer service representatives in my "quest" to get the desired results. I didn't see these people as human beings I saw them as my personal "punching bags" to vent my anger.

Fortunately for me, my husband confronted me with my horrid behavior. For many years my husband worked in customer service. After witnessing one of my "tirades" against a customer service representative, he said to me, "If one of my customers talked to me the way you just talked to that girl, I would not help her!" His comment hit me like a cold bucket of water!

I since have adopted a kinder more loving attitude in dealing with others. I strive to be more kind and loving towards *everyone* not just my family and friends. Being a kind and loving person makes you a nicer person to be around. It even makes it nicer for you to be around yourself. Since you can't get "away" from yourself you might as well make yourself nice to be around.

BE HONEST

With the introduction of "situation ethics" into our culture, honesty and integrity have become open to "interpretation." It has become okay to lie in certain situations and under certain circumstances. I simply do not agree with this philosophy. Even though there may be extreme situations where being less than truthful could save your life, "situation ethics" is not an excuse for compromising your honesty and integrity in most every day situations in which you will find yourself. By "honesty" I mean being truthful in word and in deed and by "integrity" I mean doing what you say you will do.

In America in generations past, it was understood that if a man (or woman) gave his (or her) word, you could count on it. It saddens me that for the most part, that is not the case anymore. Be that as it may, it is still not an excuse for you personally to "follow the crowd" and be less than honest yourself.

Resolve to be a person of honesty and integrity. Not just in big things but in little things as well. If you tell someone you are going to be at a certain place at a certain time and you are delayed for any reason, call that person to say you are running late and when you expect to be there. If something happens and you can't make it at all, don't just "blow it off," call and let that person know you won't be coming.

Don't say things you don't mean just to be "polite." For example, don't tell someone that you would like to get together for lunch sometime if you have no intention of ever getting together with that person for lunch. Don't tell another woman you just "love" her dress if you think it is the ugliest thing you have ever seen. It is better not to say anything at all than to spout shallow "niceties" for the sake of conversation. Don't be a superficial, two-dimensional person. Say what you mean and mean what you say. Stand by your word and if you say something, follow through with it. I am not suggesting that you be "brutally" honest here. Don't say "truthful" things that you know will hurt a person's feelings. You can be honest without being mean. You just have to think about it and use some tact and diplomacy. If you're not good at this, then you can learn.[49]

Work on developing the reputation of always doing what you say you will do. Keep the promises you make and don't make promises you can't keep. Don't get discouraged if others don't stand by their word. You are not responsible for them. You are only responsible for yourself. If you are a person of honesty and integrity that is one more person in the world who is and you have just made the world a better place to live in.

BE PATIENT

This is a tough one for a lot of us. There is even a saying you may have heard, "God give me patience and give it to me right now!" [50] I think that patience is particularly difficult for us to learn because we live in a "fast food," instant-gratification world. We are bombarded with advertising that tells us to "buy now, pay later." It seems that everything around us is telling us "Now, now, now." We don't get much practice waiting for much of anything, except maybe for traffic or to see the doctor or to check out at the store. When we are kept waiting (like in those situations mentioned above), we get stressed out and anxious and lose our "cool" very quickly.

Learn how to slow down and not be in such a hurry all the time. Life is short and it seems even shorter if we are rushing around and expecting everything to happen on a fast track time schedule. It is very difficult to be patient when your life is so crammed full of "activities" that you don't have time to wait for anything. If you can learn to slow down, it will make it easier for you to be patient with yourself and with others as well.

If you have to be somewhere at a certain time and you know you could run into traffic delays along the way, leave early enough so you can get there on time even if you get stuck in traffic. Don't set yourself up to be impatient. Think things through ahead of time and plan accordingly. Even when you plan ahead and the traffic delay is longer than you could ever have anticipated and you are sitting in traffic knowing you will be late, be patient anyway! Will letting yourself be anxious, stressed out and ticked off get you there any quicker? [51] No! Not only that, but allowing yourself to be stressed out and upset could very likely shorten your life or make you sick or both.

Another suggestion is to take a long, leisurely bath in the evening before you go to bed instead of rushing to take a shower in the morning. This will give you time to relax and think and make it easier for you to be patient.

To help you develop patience with others, remember you are not a perfect person yourself so don't expect others to be perfect. I am reminded of a bumper sticker I saw once which said, "Be patient, God isn't finished with me yet!" [52] Try to keep this in mind and maybe it will help you to be patient with others when it would be easier to just get frustrated.

UNDERSTAND THE DIFFERENCES BETWEEN MEN AND WOMEN

When I was in my twenties I thought the differences between men and women were primarily physical. I later found out that this was not the case at all. The differences between men and women go way beyond the obvious, physical differences. These differences are far-reaching and profound.

Be aware that the number one thing . . . on most men's minds most of the time is sex!

If you ever want to have a successful, healthy relationship with a man, it is important for you to have an understanding of these differences. It is a big mistake to think any man will think act or perceive things in any situation the way that you do. The more you understand about how men think and what makes them "tick" the better chance you will have in establishing a life long, happy relationship. There are several good books that explain the differences between men and women.[53]

Learn all you can about how men think and what motivates them. Be aware that the number one thing on most men's minds most of the time is sex.

You may not like it, but that is just the way it is. It is unrealistic to think you will ever change or modify that characteristic in a man. That is the way men are made. I don't understand why men are that way, but I do understand that is how most men are. More on this later when we talk about doing what it takes to make a relationship last a lifetime.

Introduction To Sections Two And Three

I feel that the next two sections need an introduction of their own. To help you understand where I am coming from, it is necessary to get an historical perspective here. Marriage based on "love" and "romance" is a fairly recent development, historically speaking. Traditionally marriage has been a contract and the purpose of marriage in the past has been very different than what it is today.

For thousands of years, marriage was a contract between a man and a woman that had to do with economics and survival and sometimes politics but seldom was "love" or "romance" even a consideration. If a husband and wife ended up being "in love" or even "friends" it was a bonus. For the most part, there simply was not the expectation that a husband and wife would love each other.

One of the purposes of marriage for the woman was to provide her a means of support. It wasn't that long ago that women stayed at home and were supported by their fathers until they married and were supported by their husbands. The idea of women being self-supporting is only two or three generations old. Sure, there was the exceptional "spinster" or "old maid" schoolteacher, but for the most part, women depended on men for their support.

Things are very different today and in most cases, love

and happiness are an expectation of marriage. Since it has only been a short time (relatively speaking) that people have been selecting their own mates with the idea of love and happiness, there isn't a long history of "successful" marriages for us to look at based on these new expectations. We are pretty much left on our own with not much to go on in regards to the best way to go about selecting a mate for a relationship that will be happy and last a lifetime.

With divorce being at such an astonishingly high rate for the past two generations, there are few people who can find out from their parents how to find the right person and have a successful marriage based on love and happiness. Also, this is not a subject that is really taught anywhere on a large scale that I know of. We are left to romance novels, television and movies for information on how to have a happy marriage, and those sources are seriously flawed and unrealistic at best.

I do not claim to have all the answers. However, because I have been down the "wrong road" many times in regards to marriage and finally found the "right road," I believe I have some useful ideas that will keep you from making the same mistakes I did and help you to find the right person and establish a happy, loving, lifelong relationship the first time around.

SECTION TWO
HOW TO FIND THE RIGHT PERSON

Chapter 5

A Few Pointers

DON'T GO LOOKING FOR HIM

As ironic as it may seem, the best way to find the right man for you is *not* to go "looking" for him. What I mean by this is don't go places or get involved in certain activities with the express purpose of "finding a man." I don't understand the process fully myself, but I do know from experience that if you are intently "looking" for a man, even though you may "find" a man, you will not be open to the right man. Perhaps you put off a different kind of "vibration" when you are "looking" that will actually repel the right man. Whatever it is, you have a better chance of finding the right man for you if you aren't "looking" for him. It is like what Henry David Thoreau said about success, "Success usually comes to those who are too busy to be looking for it." The same thing is true about a relationship with a man.

It is much better to attract a man naturally by just being yourself and doing what you enjoy than it is to conduct a full-scale "man hunt." If you are involved in pursuits and activities that will help you be the best person you can be then you will know when the right man comes along. You won't have to look for him; he will just be there.

CONCENTRATE ON IMPROVING YOURSELF

You may be thinking at this point, "Whoa, déjà vu! Didn't I already read about this in chapter four?" The answer is "yes" and I refer you back to that chapter. Here I would like to expand on why this is important in attracting the right man into your life.

Since in Chapter 4 I already discussed the kinds of things you might do to improve yourself I won't go into them again here. You can look back if you need to refresh your memory. The point is to choose something that really interests you and you can be passionate about. Don't make your decision based on where you think you will find the most men. You're not supposed to be looking for a man, remember?

Don't make your decision based on . . . where you think you will find the most men!

On the other hand, don't restrict your activities to those where you will only be with other women. Think about it; if you spend all of your free time just around other women, how do expect to attract a man? What you need is balance here. While you are not to go actively looking for a man, don't cloister yourself away from men either. You're not likely to attract the right man if you live the life of a nun.

Most of the outside activities suggested in chapter four are activities where you would most likely be around men and women, unless you take an all-woman class or join an all-woman health club or gym. You can do that if you like, but I wouldn't recommend it unless you just aren't ready to meet the right man yet.

You may be thinking, "I don't have enough free time to get involved in any of those activities suggested in chapter four." Look at how you spend your free time. How many hours per week do you watch television? Is what you are watching feeding your mind and your soul and helping you to be a better person? Or, is what you are watching just so much "junk food" for the mind? Since there is not much on television anymore that does feed the mind and soul, the answer is probably the latter. My suggestion is to turn off the "tube" and spend your time in self-improvement instead. I am not asking you to do anything I haven't done myself. Four years ago I moved to the mountains with my husband to an area where

> You're not likely to attract the right man . . .
>
> if you live the life of a nun.

there is no television signal (without the use of a satellite dish). Since we don't see the value in paying for a satellite dish, we haven't watched programmed television for three years now. I can report that we don't miss it and we have a lot more time to do more important things now. Besides, how good do you think your chances are of attracting the right man if you are a "couch potato" in front of the TV all the time?

If you are sincerely involved in something that interests you and that will help you to improve as a person then the men you will meet will more likely have something in common with you right from the start. One final note; bars and nightclubs are *not* the best place to meet men for a serious, lifelong relationship.

MAKE FRIENDS (MALE AND FEMALE)

While you are involved in improving yourself, make friends with people you meet, both men and women. Here again, it is important to have a balance in your life. Divide your time between your male and female friends. Don't spend all of your time with just other women or just with men.

You don't have to "date" every man you find interesting or who is attracted to you. Work more on developing friendships than dating relationships. I once had a male friend who told me, "Girlfriends are a dime a dozen, but real (female) friends are hard to find." If you concentrate on forming friendships then you will be laying the foundation for a lifetime romantic relationship as well. Romantic relationships that start out as friendships always have a better chance of success. After all, we are talking about ultimately finding a man to spend the rest of your life with. Wouldn't it be nicer if the two of you were friends first? I am reminded of what Jeremy Taylor said, "Love is friendship set on fire."

KEEP YOUR EYES AND YOUR HEART OPEN

What I mean by this is to not go around with virtual "blinders" on. Be aware and interested in those around you. Notice people (both men and women) and get to know them. Our fast-paced, rush, rush, rush world has conditioned most of us to be so focused on the next place we have to be or the next thing we have to do that we miss much of what goes on around us. We also miss the people who are around us as well. Slow down long enough to notice those around you. Most of them are probably nice people and you can never have too many friends.

Allow others to get to know you as well. Don't hide behind an emotional "wall." I don't mean for you to go to the opposite extreme and make yourself completely vulnerable either. Balance is always the key. If you give yourself time to get to know people, you will know whom you can trust and whom you cannot trust. Over time, you will weed out the people you can't trust and remain friends with those you can. Obviously, the man you will eventually marry needs to be someone you trust.

Chapter 6

Watch Your Behavior

BE YOURSELF WITH MEN WHO ARE ATTRACTED TO YOU

I cannot stress this enough! It is so important for you to *not* all of a sudden pretend to be someone you are not when you realize a man is attracted to you. Just be yourself. Don't go out of your way to try to impress him. If he is attracted to you then *be* who you are.

I had an important revelation at the age of fourteen. I was trying to figure out the best way to act around boys I thought were "cute." I went through the possibilities. I could be something I'm not to try to impress him, but then if he liked me that way, it wouldn't be me he liked, it would be the person I was pretending to be. Eventually I wouldn't be able to keep up the "act" and he would stop liking me because it wasn't really "me" he liked in the first place.

If I pretended to be something I'm not and he didn't like me, I would never know if he would have liked me if I had just been myself. Either way, it didn't seem to me to be a good idea to try to be anything other than my genuine self. Of course, there was always the risk that some boy I liked wouldn't like me if I was my genuine self, but if that was the case then I figured it just wasn't meant to be because it was really me he didn't like, not something I was pretending to be.

I still believe this to be an important revelation and I share it with you. The point is, don't try to anticipate what kind of woman he wants you to be and pretend to be that. It's never worth it and it never works out when you do that. Be yourself and if he doesn't like you the way you are then that's the first "clue" he's not the "one."

I recall dating a very handsome, young man when I was in my mid-twenties. I was a size ten (which was optimal for me at the time) but he wanted me to be a size three. That was never going to happen because my bones alone are bigger than a size three. He kept bugging me to lose weight when I wasn't "overweight" in the first place. I finally came to the conclusion (I don't know what took me so long) that he wanted me to be something I was not, nor ever could be, and we went our separate ways.

Don't worry. When the right man comes along, he will like you for who and what you are. You won't have to try to impress him. Just you being yourself will impress him.

DON'T PLAY "GAMES"

I'm not talking about the kind of games we play for recreation. I'm taking about emotional/psychological head games. Let me be more specific. One of the "games" woman are taught to play in our culture is "Hard to Get." This is where you do things like:

1) Make him call you three times for every one time you return his calls.
2) Tell him you are unavailable (when that is not the case) in order to make him want you more.
3) Pretend to be less interested in him than you really are.
4) In short, make him work very hard to "win" your "hand."

Then there's the "Make Him Jealous" game. It goes something like this: You want him to pay more attention to you so you start flirting with someone else, hoping that he will get jealous and fight to keep you.

Or how about the "Make Him Mine" game? This is where you intentionally get pregnant in order to get him to marry you.

Another popular game is the "If You Loved Me" game. This game is played by single and married women alike. This is where you use guilt to manipulate him into getting your way. You put on a pouty face and say "If you loved me . . ." followed by whatever it is you want him to do for you.

Then there's the "All is fair in love and war" game. This is where you feel justified in pulling any kind of dirty, underhanded, manipulative trick to get him to commit to you because, as everyone knows, "All is fair in love and war!"[52] Nonsense!

This is by no means all of the emotional/psychological head games that are possible. These are only meant as examples so you know what I mean by "games." I'm sure there are many other emotional/psychological head games that I either can't think of right now or don't even know about. When I say, "don't play games," I don't just mean the ones mentioned earlier, I mean any kind of emotional/psychological head games whatsoever. If you are honest with yourself, you know when you are playing head games and when you are not.

The playing of these games (and others not mentioned here) may be socially acceptable to some, but as far as most men are concerned, playing any kind of emotional/psychological games is juvenile and underhanded. I recommend that you just not do it.

Be honest and straightforward with a man. Treat him with respect and dignity just like you expect to be treated. Playing "games" may work in the short term to get what you want, but it is not the way to develop a long-term relationship with a man.

SECTION THREE

HOW TO DETERMINE IF HE IS THE RIGHT PERSON FOR YOU

Chapter 7

Getting Serious

GIVE YOURSELF TIME TO GET TO KNOW HIM

Oh, the pain and heartache I could have saved myself if I had just done this one thing! I accepted a proposal from one of my husbands just three weeks after we met and we were married a week later. Please don't make the same mistake I did.

Take time to get to know him. You can't know if a man is right for you in just a few weeks or even a few months. It takes time for you to know each other and develop the foundation necessary for a lifetime relationship. "Whirlwind" romances seldom last a lifetime.

You may think that after six to eight months you know each other well enough to get "engaged." My recommendation is, don't rush it. Take as much time as you need to be sure that this is really the man with whom you want to spend the rest of your life. It is better to date a long time and stay married than rush into it and get divorced later.

How much time is enough time? I can't really answer that except to say I know it is longer than a month or two, and certainly longer than three weeks! Just to give you a general guideline, I would recommend at least a year (before you even get engaged) or longer if you can. Part of this depends on how old you are when you start seeing each other. If you are only sixteen (or younger) you may want to wait until you are twenty or twenty-one before you start thinking about getting married. If you are in your early twenties then you still have plenty of time to get to know each other before even considering marriage.

No matter how you may feel, the truth is the older you are and the more life experience you have, the better your judgment will be in selecting a mate. If you are in your late twenties or older, you may not want to take several years getting to know each other before getting married. Whatever your age, my experience tells me that you simply can't know if he is the right person for you in much less than a year. Your heart may be telling you, "I love him and I can't live without him" but use your head here. We are not talking about a romantic weekend get-away, we are talking about the rest of your life, so take some time to think about it and get to know each other.

Chapter 8

Determine If You Are Compatible

One of the things I have discovered that is very important to a happy, healthy marriage is compatibility. I don't mean that you both have to be exactly alike. In fact, quite often if you are too much alike, you won't be compatible. You need to be alike enough to get along with each other but different enough to make it interesting. It also helps if areas where you are different complement each other.

Next you will find some questions and topics to think about and discuss with your boyfriend that will help you determine if you are compatible and if you complement each other. It is important for you to be as honest as possible in your answers and in your discussion. If you are less than honest, this will not help you. The objective of this is to help you find out if the man you are dating is someone you could live with for a lifetime. If you "cheat" on this, and tell him what you think he wants to hear, you may be setting yourself up to be just another divorce statistic. Sometimes it takes a lot of courage to be really honest. I urge you to do so. It will be worth it in the long run.

COMPATIBILITY QUESTIONS TO THINK ABOUT AND TOPICS TO DISCUSS WITH YOUR BOYFRIEND

These questions and topics are rather extensive, but they may not cover everything. The purpose of this is to get you to think about different areas of your lives and look at how compatible and well matched you are. I hope that when both of you have thought about these questions and topics, it will spark discussion. I also hope that if there are any problem areas, discussing these areas will bring them to light so you can look at them closely and make some wise decisions. Yes, it is sometimes uncomfortable to be made aware of problems, but if you don't know about them, you can't solve them. If you uncover any unsolvable problems, it is better to know this before you get married. "Breaking up" is traumatic, but not as traumatic as divorce, especially when there are children involved.

FAMILY AND FRIENDS

You may be wondering what family and friends have to do with compatibility. After all, you are dating your boyfriend not his family or friends, right? And he is dating you, not your family or friends. Well, the answer to that is both "yes" and "no." "Yes," you are dating each other, not your family or friends, but "no," you are not living in a "bubble." If you are considering a lifetime relationship, your family and friends *do* figure into the picture.

How close each of you is to your respective families is an important consideration. If you are really close to your family and they can't stand your boyfriend or he can't stand them or both, this could be a problem later on. The same applies if that is the case with you and your boyfriend's family. I mention this because I have known couples who were really in love be broken up by either her family or his family. Think about this and consider all the possibilities ahead of time. It is better to split up over family when you are dating (or even engaged) than to allow his or your family to break up a marriage.

Friends can be just as important as family. To some people, friends are even more important than family. If all of your friends tell you that your boyfriend is a "jerk" or he treats you like "dirt," you may want to take a closer look at your boyfriend and your relationship and re-evaluate things. If your boyfriend ever tells you that you are too good for him and he doesn't deserve you, believe him! Such a statement is a sign of a very low self-esteem. On the other hand, if you feel your boyfriend is too good for you, then you may be the one with the self-esteem problem. Either way, a relationship where either of you thinks that the other one is "too good" for you is not off to a very good start. If this is the case, chances are very high that you are not right for each other.

If you don't like any of your boyfriend's friends or they don't like you, again, take a closer look. After all, there is some merit to the saying, "Birds of a feather will gather together." [54] If his friends have undesirable characteristics, it may be you are "blinded" by love and are overlooking some of your boyfriend's characteristics that may be a problem later on.

If you are serious about each other and you haven't met his family or friends yet, this should cause you to wonder. There may be a very good reason why you haven't met his family; they may live in another state or even another country. Even if that is the case, you could always talk with them on the phone. I can't think of any good reason why you would not meet your boyfriend's friends, unless he doesn't have any. If he doesn't even have one friend, that alone should make you wonder about him.

The only reason I mention this at all is, I personally know about three or four women who have married a man (not the same one, of course) when they never met his family or friends, only to find out later that he was also married to someone else (at the same time) in another city or even another state!

You may be thinking, "There are laws against that. A man couldn't do that." Well, yes there are laws against that, but that doesn't mean a man couldn't and wouldn't do it anyway. If you really want something to think about, go rent the movie, *Deceived* [55] (if you can find it). Sure, it is only a movie, but where do you think they got the idea? Things like that do happen. Just be careful and make sure it doesn't happen to you.

Why do you think we have the saying, "Love is blind"?[56] It is because when we are "in love" we tend to overlook things in the other person and sometimes miss the obvious. One of the reasons for this book is to help you to take off the "blinders" of love and really take a good look at this man you are considering as a lifetime mate.

In talking about family, I want to take a few moments to address a family issue for single mothers. So, if you don't have children, you can skip to the next topic of "Lifestyle." If you have one or more children, it is important to exercise the proper timing in introducing them to someone you are dating.

I learned this lesson the hard way. I would like to pass on to you the lesson I learned so you don't have to put yourself and your child(ren) through what I went through with my child.

My son's father and I separated and started divorce proceedings when my son was six months old. When my son was about fourteen months old, I started dating someone who was kind and gentle and loved children. I introduced him to my son a short time after we started dating. Since I was on a limited budget, and my new boyfriend loved children, we would often do things together that included my son. My son loved playing with my boyfriend and I was happy that the two of them got along so well together.

My boyfriend and I dated for about four months. This was enough time for my son to become attached to my boyfriend. Things did not work out in our relationship and we broke up. My son could not understand why the nice man who played with him stopped coming over. He became depressed for a time over losing this friend he had made. I was angry with myself that I had exposed my son to such a thing. It was then that I understood how important it was to protect my son from such loss. I could handle the breakup of a relationship, but I realized that it was not fair to make my son go through the emotional trauma of losing one friend after another as my dating relationships broke up. I resolved to be more cautious in the future about introducing my dates to my son. I decided that it was better to pay a babysitter and wait until my dating relationship was on a more firm foundation before I brought my son into the picture.

For the sake of your children, please exercise caution and use common sense when it comes to introducing your children to men you are dating. It is wise to wait until you are fairly sure of the relationship before allowing your children to spend much time with your boyfriend.

LIFESTYLE

In considering your level of compatibility it is important to consider what kind of lifestyle you each have and what kind of lifestyle you plan to have as a married couple. If each of you has a very different kind of idea about what kind of lifestyle you want to live, this could cause serious problems in the relationship in the future.

What do I mean by lifestyle? Lifestyle encompasses many things. First of all think about where each of you would like to live. Do you want to live in a big metropolitan area, or a medium-size city, or a small town? Would you rather live in the suburbs? Do you prefer a very small community or even rural living? If your dream is to live in the country, how much property do you want to live on? Would you enjoy living on a farm or a ranch?

Do you want to live in an apartment or a condo the rest of your life? Do you hope to own your own single family home someday? These are things that are important to discuss. If one of you loves the hustle, bustle and excitement of the big city and the other one longs to live in the peace and tranquility of the country and you can't come to a compromise that is acceptable to both of you, then this could be an unsolvable problem.

What states would you consider living in? Are there any states you would definitely not want to live in? Would you consider living in another country? Are there any countries you would not ever want to live in under any circumstances? I have lived in ten different states all over the U.S. My husband has lived in several countries all over the world. There are some states and some countries where neither of us would consider living. Fortunately for us, they are the same states and countries.

Talk about this with your boyfriend. If his idea of the perfect life is to live on a horse ranch in Montana and your idea of the perfect life is a beach house in Florida, you need to know about this before you make a lifetime commitment. If you would love to be a missionary in a foreign country and your boyfriend would not live outside the U.S. under any circumstances, again this is something you both need to know about. There may be times when both of you will have to live somewhere you would prefer not to live. He may get a promotion that requires the family move to a certain state or country, or that may happen to you, for that matter. The point is, when you do have a choice, what will your choices be and are they compatible? When you don't have a choice are you willing to be flexible?

I know of a married couple that was living in the same city as her parents. The husband got a job transfer to another state. She refused to go with him because she could not bear the thought of living away from her parents. He took the job and flew home on the weekends as much as possible. This went on for a couple of years. He finally met someone and fell in love. She had an affair and got pregnant. As you might imagine, they ended up getting divorced. I'm sure you have heard the saying "absence makes the heart grow fonder."[57] While this may be true if the absence is short, a long absence will quite often make the heart grow fonder of someone else!

While you can't know all the things that may happen in the future, it is a good idea to discuss how you feel about living in the same town as your parents or his parents. Also discuss how you feel about relocating and if you would be willing to do so if one of you did get a job transfer. Which of your jobs or careers will take priority? Are you willing to compromise? I knew of some couples in the Air Force who would get married in order to be able to live off base. Their agreement was to stay married until "PCS (Permanent Change of Station) do us part." In other words, as soon as one of them got orders to another duty station, they would get divorced!

Needless to say, that is not the way to set up a lifetime

relationship. If each of you plans on pursuing a career that could take you in opposite directions, you need to figure out what you plan to do in any given situation before you "walk down the aisle."

Another aspect of lifestyle is your family background and how you were raised. Was your family poor, lower middle class, middle class, upper middle class, wealthy, filthy rich? The kind of family you were raised in influences your outlook on life. If you came from a family who didn't have much (like I did) then you probably learned to watch money very closely and work hard for everything you have. If your boyfriend came from a family that always had lots of money and he never had to work hard for anything, you may have very different value systems and ideas about money.

Maybe the reverse is true. Perhaps you came from a family that gave you everything you ever wanted and you never had to work for anything. And perhaps your boyfriend came from a lower class family where he learned at an early age that if he wanted something, he would have to work hard and earn it. He may not understand you spending the day "shopping" and spending $1,000 or more on new clothes.

He also may not understand why you have to buy a new evening gown every time you get invited to a party. While love stories abound about people from different levels of society falling in love, this can also cause a great amount of tension in a relationship. If you do come from very different family backgrounds, it is important to be aware that this can be a source of friction.

If the relationship is going to succeed, you both need to be sensitive to the feelings and perceptions of each other and be willing to make whatever adjustments are necessary for the relationship to work. The closer your family backgrounds are, the easier it will be for you to understand where the other person is coming from.

If you do come from similar family backgrounds it is important not to assume that you have exactly the same values and ideas about family, work, money, etc. Talk about these subjects. If you do get married, will both of you work? Who will take care of the household chores? Do either of you think there are certain things that are "men's work" and "women's work"? Do you agree? How does each of you think that money should be spent? Do you plan on having separate checking accounts? Do you plan to have a joint checking account? If you have a joint account, which one of you will manage it? Which one of you will pay the bills and handle the finances? According to statistics, a high percentage of marriages break up over disagreements about money. To avoid this happening to you, be sure you discuss the money issue fully and come to some agreements while you are in the dating or engagement stage.

> He may not understand you spending the day "shopping" . . . and spending $1,000 or more on new clothes.

Also included in lifestyle is recreation and hobbies. How do each of you choose to spend your free time? Do you enjoy spectator sports like football, baseball, soccer, basketball, hockey, etc.? Do you participate in any sports? If so, which ones? Are you an amusement park fan? Are you a movie buff? Do you spend your free time reading? Do you like to make things? Are you into photography, painting, sculpting, ceramics, crafts, etc.? Do you spend a lot of time watching television? Are there certain TV programs that you just can't

> If you love sailing and he gets seasick . . .
>
> You may not be compatible in this area!

miss? If he is an avid rock and mountain climber and you have a fear of heights, or if you love sailing and he gets seasick, you may not be compatible in this area. I'm not saying that you have to do everything together, but the more things you like to do together, the better.

Only the two of you can decide if any difference you have could be serious enough to be a threat to the relationship. The point is to talk about what you like to do and find things you like to do together. Don't be like the main character in *Runaway Bride* [58] and "like" everything he likes in order to "make" him like you. As mentioned earlier, be yourself and let him know what you like to do for recreation and find out what he likes to do for recreation. If the differences are too great, you're probably not meant for each other.

Think about it; if you both work in separate places and you spend your free time doing different things, how do you expect to build a life together? If he is off hunting with the "boys" or watching sports on TV with the "guys" while you are at the gym with the "girls" or hang-gliding with your friends what do you have in common? Please don't misunderstand me. I'm not saying that the two of you can't do separate things with your friends sometimes. What I am saying is if all or most of your free time is spent apart, then it is difficult to build a relationship that will last. In order to stay together you need to spend time together. Find out what your common interests are and spend time doing the things you both enjoy doing.

While on the subject of how you spend your free time, I would like to bring your attention to your respective preferences in music. What kind of music do you like? What kind of music does he like? Do you like to listen to the same kinds of music? Is there any music that you like that he doesn't like? Is there any kind of music he likes that you don't like? While you may think that music preference is a minor thing, it could be a big problem in your relationship if one of you just loves to listen to a kind of music that the other one can't stand. The more you have in common in your taste in music, the better.

The final subject I would like to discuss in regards to lifestyle is pets. As I'm sure you know, some people like pets and some do not. Even when people do like pets, different people have different preferences as to the pets they keep. There are "dog" people, "cat" people, "horse" people, etc. It is important to discuss with your boyfriend what each of you thinks about pets. If you love cats and he either hates cats or is allergic to them, this could be a problem unless you decide you can live without cats being a part of your life. If you have a spider phobia and he wants to have a tarantula as a pet this could spell "trouble." It would be impossible for me to list all the possible pet scenarios here. The point is, talk about your ideas and preferences in pets. I have known people who are so attached to their pets that if a prospective mate would not accept their pets, there is no hope of them ever getting together.

FOOD AND HEALTH

Since once you are married you will be eating most of your meals together, it is important for you to have some level of compatibility in this area. Let him know what kinds of foods you like and find out what kinds of foods he likes. If you are a "health food nut" and he is "hooked" on "junk food," this could be a problem. The same is true if it is the other way around. Not only is it important to have some level of compatibility on what kinds of foods you like, it is also important to be compatible in your attitudes about food. If one of you thinks food is for nourishment and the other one thinks food is for comfort or reward, this could cause a problem. If one of you is a strict vegetarian and the other is strictly a "meat and potatoes" kind of person, and neither of you is willing to change, you are not compatible in this area.

Even though a certain level of compatibility is desirable, it is not necessary for you to both like all the same foods in order to have a successful relationship. For example, my husband is allergic to onion and garlic oil. I love onions and garlic. We have compromised. We found out that while he can't eat fresh (or freshly cooked) onions or garlic, he can eat onion or garlic powder. So, instead of using fresh onion or garlic in cooking (or going without it completely), I use onion and garlic powder in dishes that call for onions or garlic.

Another example is, my husband likes beef but I can't digest beef. Rather than me cooking two separate meat dishes at home, he waits until we eat out at a restaurant where he can order beef and I can order something else.

Once you are aware of where you are compatible and where you are not as far as food is concerned, you can discuss where you are willing to make changes or compromise in order to make the relationship work.

What you eat is directly related to your health. If one of you is careful about eating food that is good for you and promotes good health and the other only cares about how food tastes and cares nothing about if it is good for you or not, then this could be a problem.

Talk about your attitudes regarding food and health. Find out how compatible you are. The more you have in common in this area, the better.

PERSONAL HABITS

If you are considering a long-term relationship, it is important to be aware of each other's personal habits. Each of us has a multitude of habits that are so familiar to us that we don't even think about them. However, the habits we engage in unconsciously could be the very thing that drives another person crazy.

Don't make the mistake of believing that just because you love someone, you can necessarily overlook habits he might have that you find irritating. This goes both ways.

Know enough about each other so you know what each other's personal habits are and talk about any habits that either of you have that "bug" the other one. Is there anything that he does that either bugs you or drives you crazy? Is there anything that you do that either bugs him or drives him crazy? Be open and honest about this. If there is something he does that really bothers you, silently believing, "I love him so much that I will get used to it," is a mistake. In most cases, not only will you *not* get used to "it" but more likely than not, "it" will bother you more and more the longer you are together. The reverse is true if you have habits that really bother him.

Just in case you aren't sure what I mean by "personal habits" I will name a few as examples. This is not a comprehensive list by any means; it only serves as an example to get you thinking in the right direction. Habits that others may find irritating include nail biting, smoking, gum popping, finger drumming, lip smacking (while eating), laughing with a snort, fidgeting, obsessive-compulsive behaviors, hair twisting, mustache or beard stroking, knuckle cracking, interrupting, constantly correcting the other person, nagging, finding fault, blaming others, always needing to have the last word, gossiping, overeating, just to mention a few.

Another mistake that people who are "in love" often make is believing that if there are habits they don't like in the other person, they will be able to change that person to their liking. I have learned from bitter experience that you can never change another person. You can only change yourself. If you don't like him just the way he is, then maybe he's not the right one for you. If he doesn't like you just the way you are, then maybe you're not the right one for him. People do change over time in a relationship, but the change comes internally from within, not externally from without. Love will get you to do a lot of things, but only those things you choose to do yourself, not things that are forced on you by the other person. My husband and I have grown more compatible over the length of our relationship, but he has changed himself and I have changed myself, we have not changed each other.

One question for you to ask yourself is, "Is there anything he does that I can't live with?" He needs to ask the same question about you. If the answer for either of you is "yes" then this needs to be resolved if you hope to build a lasting relationship. An external "promise" of "Oh, yes I will change that for you, Baby" is not going to cut it. As I mentioned earlier, change comes from within. Anyone can quit doing something for a short time, but truly changing a bad habit takes time and a lot of work. If you believe the "promise" is genuine, give it plenty of time to tell that it is.

I broke up with my first husband several times while we were dating because of his smoking and excessive drinking. He would always come back to me with the promise that he would quit smoking and drinking. He did quit, for a while, but he always went back to his bad habits sooner or later. His "promise" was only a manipulation to get me to come back. Please don't make the same mistake I did.

RACE AND ETHNIC BACKGROUND

This is a sensitive area; however, I feel I would be remiss if I did not cover it. Personally, I have no problem at all with people from different racial or ethnic backgrounds being together. Sadly, there are too many people in the world who still do have a very big problem with racially mixed couples, so if you are a racially mixed couple, unless you plan to live isolated from the rest of the world, you will have to deal with them.

People can be very cruel and it is important for you to be aware that there are still racial "hate groups" that are very active in this country. No matter how much you may love each other, the hate and interference of others could tear you apart unless you are aware of what could happen and are prepared to deal with it.

If you are a racially mixed couple it might be a good idea to find out where there are the most people who are accepting of such relationships and plan to live there. I know from my experience that some states and cities would be easier to live in as a racially mixed couple than others. For example, I have lived in California and for the most part, people don't seem to bother racially mixed couples or try to give them a hard time. That may not be true in all parts of California, but it is true in many parts of California. On the other hand, I have also lived in the Deep South where a racially mixed couple is likely to be harassed on a regular basis.

The important thing is to know what you are up against and prepare yourselves to deal with it. If you truly do love each other, than make a pact with each other that you will not let racial differences come between you. You also need to be very sensitive to the feelings of each other and never make an issue of your racial differences.

If you do not believe you can deal with the possible pressures that others may put on you or you do not believe you can leave race out of all of your arguments, perhaps it is not wise for you to consider a long-term relationship with a person from another race. It is naive to believe that an interracial relationship won't have its own special challenges. As the old saying goes, "if you can't take the heat, get out of the kitchen!"[59]

If you are considering a long-term relationship with someone from a different race, I suggest you do some further reading on the subject.[60]

RELIGIOUS BELIEFS AND PHILOSOPHY

This is another sensitive area that I feel needs to be addressed. To have a successful, long-term relationship, it is important for a couple to be closely aligned in what they believe about spiritual things. It is not likely that you would even be attracted to someone who is completely opposite from you in this area, although, I suppose it is possible.

The point here is, the closer you are in your religious beliefs and philosophy, the better. Do not assume that just because he is a member of the same religious group as you that you are compatible. There are often many differing philosophies within the same religious group. For example, there are many different sects of Jews with widely different beliefs and practices. Just because two people belong to the

Jewish faith does not necessarily mean they are compatible in this area.

The same thing is true of Christianity. The last I did any research in this area there were hundreds of different "denominations" of Christianity. Each of them has different beliefs. For example if one of you is Catholic and the other one is Baptist, you may have difficulty getting along with each other when it comes to religion, especially if each of you is strong in his or her beliefs.

It is a mistake as well to assume that you are compatible in the area of religion just because you both belong to the same denomination. Even people within the same denomination can have conflicting beliefs. For example, I know some Christians who focus on the negative side of Christianity. They only see how wretched and worthless they are compared to God and they often talk about how they are nothing but "filthy rags" without Jesus. While it is true that God made us and we would not be here if it wasn't for Him, there are others (myself included) who prefer to focus on the positive side of Christianity and see all the good things God has done, and be grateful for God's love that sent His Son to die for the lost so that those who accept Him as their Savior can spend eternity with Him in Heaven. My point is, the "negative" Christians see themselves as worthless "filthy rags" while the "positive" Christians see themselves as redeemed children of the King. The only way for you to know if you are compatible with each other in this area is for you to get to know each other and talk with each other about your beliefs. Some people have the philosophy that one's religious beliefs are private and do not need to be discussed with anyone else. While it is true that one's beliefs are a private matter, if you plan living your life with another person, it is crucial that you be in agreement on a spiritual level.

If you are dating someone with religious beliefs different from yours, you may believe, "We love each other so much, we can each believe whatever we want, it won't interfere with our relationship." However, if you get serious about each other and decide to marry, you can become painfully aware of your religious differences once you start planning a wedding.

My husband and I were professional wedding photographers for three years. During that time we photographed many different kinds of weddings. Each religious group has a different idea about how a wedding ceremony should be conducted and the rituals that are to be observed. Keep in mind that when it comes to what kind of wedding you are going to have, it is not just the two of you that you need to consider; there is your family and his family as well. We talked about the importance of family in an earlier chapter.

Religious differences become even more visible when you start talking about raising a family. I have known some couples that have different religious beliefs and decide to "compromise" and teach their children both the faith of the mother and faith of the father and then let the children decide what they want to believe. This can be very confusing to children and I would not recommend this approach. It is much better if you are compatible in your religious beliefs. Then you won't have to make any religious "compromises" at all.

There are a couple of exceptions that I would like to mention here. Please do not believe that if you are in agreement on spiritual matters that you can ignore all other areas of compatibility. I made this mistake with two of my husbands.

My second husband and I met at church and he had the aspiration of becoming a preacher. I thought that since we were both Christians and went to the same church, that meant we were automatically compatible in every other way. I reasoned that since we both were following Christ, we could work out any differences we might have by asking for God's guidance and praying about it.

While I truly believe in looking to God for direction and

praying, prayer is not a substitute for making a wise choice in selecting a mate in the first place. My second husband and I only knew each other four weeks before we were married. Over time we discovered we were severely incompatible in many areas. The fact that we were both Christians and went to the same church never made up for the incompatibilities in other areas, and the relationship eventually unraveled.

My third husband was not a Christian when I met him. Through our dating relationship, I began to share my beliefs with him and eventually we began studying the Bible together. We started becoming serious about each other so I prayed that God give me a "sign" if this was the man I was supposed to marry. Instead of being still and waiting for God to pick the "sign," I decided that the "sign" from God that would mean I was supposed to marry this man was if he became a Christian. Naturally, when he did become a Christian, I took that to mean I should marry him, even though I knew in my heart I was only with him because I felt sorry for him.

We started our married life together as Christians and we attended worship together. This relationship also fell apart because it was built on a faulty foundation and because we really had nothing in common but our faith. I was so anxious to marry again that I forced the relationship and thought (again) that if we were both Christians, we could work out our differences. I made the same mistake twice just to make sure it was a mistake!

I offer you these two examples from my own experience to illustrate to you that it is most important for you to have more in common with the man you expect to marry than just your faith. The purpose of these examples is to keep you from making the same mistakes I did. You can't just take two people from the same faith (whatever that may be), put them together and expect for them to be happy for a lifetime. There is much more to it than that. So, the first exception to spiritual compatibility is, you can't expect spiritual compatibility alone to assure you of a successful relationship.

The second exception is in regards to having a relationship with someone who does not share your religious beliefs and philosophy. It is important to be very careful here. As mentioned earlier, it is preferable to be with someone who does share your religious beliefs and philosophy, however this is the exception. If one of you has very strong beliefs and the other is either neutral or not strong in his/her beliefs and is willing to allow the one who is strong in his/her beliefs to practice those beliefs without interference (this includes raising any children you may have in the faith of the one with strong beliefs), then you may be able to have a happy lifelong relationship even though you have differing beliefs.

If this is the case, I would recommend two things. First, since you differ in your religious beliefs, it is very important that you are compatible in most other areas if you expect the relationship to work. Second, it is crucial that the one with strong beliefs *not* badger or nag the other one into accepting his/her beliefs.[61] The one without strong beliefs may eventually accept the beliefs of the other, but it is a mistake to make that an expectation of the relationship. If you are not willing to accept each other just the way you are, then perhaps you are not right for each other.

POLITICAL VIEWS AND BELIEFS

Since I have been treading on sensitive ground, I may as well include this area as well. I want to make it clear that when I say it is important for you to be compatible in the area of political views and beliefs I mean much more than you both being "Republicans" or "Democrats" (or you both being members of any other "Party" for that matter).

Here are some questions for each of you to answer to spark discussion between you to determine if you are politically compatible.

- When it comes to government control over society in general and your lives in particular, what role do you believe government should have?
- Are you in favor of big government and lots of laws, rules and regulations that control society and individuals?
- Do you believe there are too many laws, rules and regulations?
- Do you believe that government should be limited? If so, to what extent should it be limited?
- Do you believe that individuals have the right to privacy?
- Do you believe that the only people who want privacy are criminals?
- Do you believe that the Constitution is still a valid document?
- Do you believe the Constitution is out of date and should be replaced?
- Do you believe our founding fathers set up a democracy in this country?
- Do you believe our founding fathers set up a republic in this country?
- Do you believe there is any difference between a republic and a democracy?
- Do you know the difference between a republic and a democracy?
- Do you support the United Nations?
- Are you in favor of a one-world government?
- Do you believe it is the responsibility of government to support those who cannot support themselves?
- Do you believe it is the responsibility of private charity to support those who cannot support themselves?
- Do you believe it is the job of government to take from those who have and give it to those who don't have?
- Are you in favor of the "Social Security" system?
- Do you believe people are individually responsible to

plan for their retirement instead of depending on the government to take care of them in their old age?
- Are you in favor of socialized medicine?
- Do you believe that the government has the right to dictate to parents how they should raise and discipline their children and what their children should be taught?
- Are you in favor of special interest groups and various "lobbies" influencing how our representatives vote and what laws are made?
- Do you believe that politics is too complicated for you to understand?
- Do you believe that liberty and freedom are worth fighting for?
- Do you believe everything your government tells you?
- Do you believe the government's tax system is fair?
- Do you believe it is the job of government to grant and withhold certain "rights" to various groups and individuals?
- Do you believe that "rights" don't come from government, but come from God?
- Do you believe life begins at conception?
- Do you believe life begins at birth?
- What are your beliefs about abortion?
- Do you believe the government should give grants to do experiments on human embryos?
- Do you believe the government should give grants to do research on human cloning?
- Do you believe that human cloning should be banned?
- Do you believe women should be sent into combat?
- Do you consider yourself politically active?
- Do you consider yourself politically passive?

This is not a comprehensive list of political questions by any means. Please feel free to use the above questions as a springboard to other political issues you may think of.

Hopefully this is enough to spark discussion between you and help you to determine if your political views and beliefs are compatible. If you end up in a big fight after discussing the above questions, that is a clue that you may not be compatible in this area.

After an in-depth political discussion with each other, you may be surprised at what you find out about each other. If you are still talking to each other after this, then congratulations, because political views and beliefs are quite often the topic of bitter disputes between couples. For this reason, if you have political views that are incompatible, it is better to find out before you make a lifelong commitment to each other.

SENSE OF HUMOR

Some people have a sense of humor . . . and see the funny side of life . . .

There are two different parts to compatibility when it comes to sense of humor. The first part is whether you have a sense of humor or not. Some people have a sense of humor and see the funny side of life while others are serious most of the time and rarely see anything funny about life at all.

A mismatch here could make both of you unhappy. The one with the sense of humor would never understand why the serious one doesn't "lighten up" and see the funny side of life. On the other hand, the serious one would be irritated that the one with the sense of humor takes things so lightly and isn't serious enough. If one of you is constantly trying to stifle the humor of the other or if one of you thinks the other is way too serious, that is a clue that perhaps you are not compatible in this area.

The second part of compatibility here is if you both have a sense of humor, what kind of sense of humor do you each have? I used to think that either you had a sense of humor or you didn't and if you had a sense of humor, it was the same as everyone else with a sense of humor. I have discovered over the years that there are many different kinds of humor and they are not all compatible.

It is important to discuss with each other what kind of sense of humor you each have and what kinds of things you each think are funny.

while others are serious most of the time . . . and rarely see anything funny about life at all!

What one person may think is funny, another may think is sick or not a subject for humor.

Let me give you an example. I dated a young man years ago. He was handsome, charming and ambitious. I thought he was quite a catch until I got to know him better. I started to realize that his sense of humor always revolved around death and dying. He would joke about things that I did not think were appropriate. Most of the time, I did not find his jokes amusing. His brand of humor made me uncomfortable and he started giving me the creeps. I finally broke up with him because I just couldn't take his morbid sense of humor.

When it comes to sense of humor, you don't have to agree on everything you each think is funny. For example I really think those silly movies like *Airplane*[62] and *Naked Gun*[63] are hilariously funny, while my husband doesn't think those kinds of movies are funny at all. There are also some things my husband thinks are funny that I don't think are funny at all. However, for the most part, my husband and I laugh about the same kinds of things and have essentially the same kind of sense of humor.

I am talking about an overall picture here, not each individual funny thing you encounter from day to day. The difference is one of degree. Some differences are to be expected, but if one of you is constantly laughing at or making jokes about something that the other one just doesn't think is funny, then you may not be compatible in this area.

PERSONALITY TYPE

There are many books on the market that talk about different personality types. Some of them describe these different types using letters as in "A" type personality "B" type personality and so forth. Others associate personality types to colors such as "Blue," "Red," "Green," etc. I have even heard of animals being associated with different personality types like "Monkey," "Lion," "Otter," etc.

It is not my purpose here to go into detail about the different types of personalities that exist. If you want specific information on this subject, there are plenty of resources.[64] My purpose here is for you to think about what personality type each of you has and determine if you are compatible.

Some personality types are compatible and complement each other, while some personality types compete with one another and are not compatible at all. When it comes to personality types, quite often if you are both the same type, you won't be compatible. It is more often two different types that complement each other. For example, I tend to be a very outgoing, hyper kind of person while my husband is more solitary, laid-back and mellow. We complement each other because he tends to calm me down some and keep me on track and I help to motivate him and bring him out of his "shell." Over the time we have been together, I have become calmer than I was when we met and he has become more outgoing than he was when we met. We tend to balance each other out and it is a good match.

The interesting thing is, I have often been attracted to men who have the same personality type as me, but I now realize that if I were with someone like that for very long, it would drive me crazy. By the same token, if my husband were with a woman who was the same personality type as he is, he would soon be bored with her.

If you don't know anything about the different personality types, I suggest you learn about them to help you determine if you are compatible and complement each other in this area.[64]

There is another aspect of personality that I would like to bring to your attention. It has been my observation that people either tend to be "early birds" or "night owls." If you expect to spend much time together, it is crucial that you both be the same here. If one of you is a night owl and

People tend to be . .

"Early Birds" or . . .

"Night Owls"!

the other is an early bird, you will either not see much of each other or one or both of you will be unhappy.

By nature, I am an early bird. I like to wake up with the sunrise and go to bed early. My husband is an early bird as well. There are times when we stay up late on special occasions, but most of the time we are "early to bed and early to rise."[65]

There were times when I was single that I worked jobs that started in the evening and ended in the wee hours of the morning, and on the weekends I would go dancing at clubs that didn't even get started until 9 P.M. I recall times when I would meet someone interesting and talk until the sun came up the next morning and then sleep the whole day, but that is not what I prefer.

Much of the social life in our culture tends to cater to night owls. If early birds (like me) want to be a part of that social life, they have to make sacrifices.

So keep in mind that just because you meet someone who is on a night owl schedule, that doesn't necessarily mean he's a night owl. He may be an early bird who just wants to be a part of the social life. On the other hand, you may be the early bird with the night owl schedule. Don't let your boyfriend mistake you for a night owl just because of your schedule.

Sometimes night owls are forced into an early bird job schedule. So just because someone gets up at 5 A.M. to get ready for work, that doesn't necessarily mean he's an early bird.

You can't just assume someone is an early bird or night owl by looking at the schedule he keeps. You need to talk about it and find out for sure. If you are either both early birds or both night owls, it will make for a much better relationship.

GENERAL OUTLOOK ON LIFE

What I mean by "general outlook on life" is how you see the world around you. What is your attitude or disposition? Are you an optimist or a pessimist? To tell the difference, maybe a quote from Sir Winston Churchill will help: "A pessimist sees the difficulty in every opportunity; an optimist sees the opportunity in every difficulty."

Some attitudes and dispositions can be quite conflicting with other attitudes and dispositions. Compare your attitude and disposition with that of your boyfriend. Are you compatible? Do you both see the world pretty much the same way? Are you radically different in the way in which you see things? Do your attitudes about life complement each other? Are your dispositions compatible? You have a much better chance for a successful relationship if you have a similar outlook on life. If you have a cheerful disposition and your boyfriend has a sour disposition, in the long run, neither of you will be happy.

My third husband and I had opposite outlooks on life. I was always looking for and seeing the good things in life and he was always seeing the bad. He resented me for being happy and cheerful most of the time and I couldn't understand why he was in such a "bummer" mood most of the time.

One time he came home from work and said that his boss wrote him up for having a "bad attitude." I didn't say anything to him, but I thought to myself, "Your boss is right! You do have a bad attitude!"

While we were married, I did everything I could think of to change his attitude from negative to positive, but as I mentioned earlier, change comes from within, not without. When we divorced after four years of marriage, he still had a negative outlook on life.

If you look at your respective outlooks on life before you

make a lifelong commitment to each other and determine your compatibility level, it will be much better than getting divorced later over not being compatible.

SEX

Couples often overlook sexual compatibility for a variety of reasons. Some couples think that sex is such a natural part of life that it is not possible to be incompatible in this area. While it is true that sex is a natural part of life, it is not true that sexual incompatibilities don't exist between men and women.

Then there are other couples that think they should wait until after they are married before they even talk about sex. To these couples I would say that if a serious sexual incompatibility is not discovered until after you are married, it is too late. If there are any serious sexual incompatibilities, you need to find that out before you "walk down the aisle."

The fact that many marriages break up over sexual issues says that this is a very important area to examine before you get married and make sure you are in agreement about sex.

I am not going to moralize here or offer advice on how to find out if you are sexually compatible or not. That is a private matter between the two of you. You are adults and are morally responsible for your actions and decisions.

The point is to find out if you are sexually compatible and be open and honest with each other. Talk about your expectations. Talk about what you will and won't do sexually. Discuss what you think is appropriate sexual behavior between a man and a woman and what is not. Don't assume anything. People have a lot of different ideas about what is and what is not appropriate in a sexual situation.

I recall reading a letter written by a new bride to an advice column. This young bride wanted to know if she should be concerned because on her wedding night, her husband wanted her to lie in a cold tub of water before they had sex and then lie perfectly still while he made love to her. The columnist replied that the husband appeared to have a very serious sexual problem and in all likelihood was a necrophiliac! (I'll let you do your own research on that one!) Something like that would definitely be good to know before your wedding night!

Unfortunately, deviant sexual behavior and sexual fetishes have become more prevalent in our society. It would be a mistake to assume that any boyfriend you might date has what you would consider "normal" ideas about sex. You won't know what his ideas about sex are unless you talk about it.

When you do talk about sex, create an atmosphere of openness and honesty. You don't want to be telling each other what you want to hear. The point is to find out your true feelings and ideas about sex. I have seen it happen all too often where a woman will lead a man to believe that she is agreeable to everything he wants sexually and then after they are married, she loses interest in sex and doesn't want to do any of the things she said she would do before they got married. It is important not to say things you don't mean. Also, only make the promises you intend to keep. In many cases, sex is more important to men than it is to women. It is not fair to him to use sex to get him to commit to you and then leave him in the cold. We will discuss this in more detail in a later chapter.

In summary, I would like to talk about counting the cost in determining if this is the right relationship for you. This is what I mean by "counting the cost." I have discovered that for everything you do in life there is a price to be paid. What you have to determine is, is the price you are paying worth what you are getting for it?

Let me give you some examples. There was a young woman who was in a terrible accident and her legs were badly damaged. The doctors said they could save her legs, but they told her mother that her daughter would never walk again. When the young woman heard this news she said that not only would she walk again, but she would dance!

Through strong will, determination and lots of physical therapy, the young woman did indeed walk again and she became a well-known dancer as well. Many years into her dancing career, she became romantically involved with a famous singer. The famous singer asked her to marry him, but as a condition of the marriage, he wanted her to give up her dancing career and stay at home and raise a family. After all this woman had gone through to be able to dance in the first place, she decided that giving up her career was too high of a price to pay to be married to this man, even though she was in love with him. She declined his proposal and continued in her dancing career. This of course is an example of the value of the marriage being less than the price demanded.

Here is another example. There are many things that I like, but not so much that I feel I can't live without them. Some of those things are horseback riding, watching professional football, watching ballet and going to basketball games. My husband doesn't care for any of those things. In having a relationship with my husband, I have agreed to virtually give up horseback riding, watching professional football, watching ballet and going to basketball games. To me, giving up those things is very much worth what I get in return. So, in this case the value of the relationship is very much worth the price I am paying for it.

The point is to consider what price you are paying to be in this relationship and then decide if what you are paying to be in the relationship is worth what you are getting out of the relationship.

Chapter 9

If He's Not The "One"

Of course, if after going through all of the areas of compatibility mentioned in this book (and any other areas that may come up in discussion), you come to the conclusion that you are not meant for each other, then the only sensible, adult thing to do is break up.

As heartbreaking as it may be for you to discover that you have serious incompatibilities that cannot be reconciled and it is best for you to break up with each other, it is much better to learn this and deal with it before you are married than after.

Just because you discover that you do not have what it takes for a successful long-term relationship, that does not mean you have to get mad at each other or hate each other in order to break up.

I remember one boyfriend I dated when I was in my mid-twenties. We went together for six months. I thought we had a positive, caring relationship. I was very much in love and was entertaining ideas of getting engaged. He did not feel the same way, however, and one day when I went to see him, he sat with me on the couch, held both of my hands, looked deep into my eyes and told me in a very kind and caring way that he thought we were going in different directions and had different expectations about life and it didn't make sense for us to continue our dating relationship.

Even though I was sad about our breakup, I have to admit that it was the kindest, most thoughtful breakup I had ever experienced up to that point. What I am trying to say is, once you realize that you are not right for each other, be kind about how you break up. Yes, you may still love each other or one of you may be in love and the other one may not be. Whatever the case may be, there is no sense in clinging to a relationship that you know in your heart has no chance of surviving in the long run. Hanging on to a doomed relationship because it is too hard to say goodbye or because "breaking up is hard to do"[66] is just a waste of time for both of you. The sooner you come to grips with reality, the sooner each of you can move on and find your soul mates.

If after you determine you are not right for each other, the first thoughts that come to your mind are, "I can't break up with him, he needs me" or "If I break up with him he will never find any one else to love him" or "I can't break up with him, I need him" or "If I break up with him I will never find any one else to love me" or anything close to those thoughts, then you definitely need to break up because your relationship is unhealthy and sitting on a faulty foundation. If you have any thoughts like the ones just mentioned, please go back and reread the first section of this book, "How to be the right person."

If you are in a relationship and determine that you are not right for each other and you are afraid to break up with your boyfriend for any reason or if you are afraid he will hurt you if you tell him you want to break up, then you are in a very unhealthy relationship and I suggest you seek professional help.[67]

SECTION FOUR

HOW TO MAKE IT LAST A LIFETIME

Chapter 10

Mates For Life

KEEP BEING THE RIGHT PERSON

You may think it is silly for me to say such a thing, but the reason I do is because I know so many people who think that as soon as they are married, their goal is reached and they can just "relax" now and not do anything. Nothing could be further from the truth!

You are never so perfect that there is not room for improvement and you never know so much that you can't learn something new. One of my husband's favorite quotes is, "The most important things you learn in life are the things you learn after you know it all."[68]

Just because you are married doesn't mean you can stop growing personally. What I mean by "keep being the right person" is to continue to strive to be the best person you can be and do your best to live up to your full potential.

Sometimes after marriage women become distracted especially after children come onto the scene. I am a mother myself and I realize that raising children is a full-time job, but that doesn't mean you have to put personal growth on "hold" until your children all graduate from college. There is always some way in which you can keep improving yourself and learn how to be a better person, even if it is only reading a book while the baby is taking a nap.

The other thing I would like to mention about children is your children are *not* yours to keep. Children are a gift from God. Your job as a mother is to care for them, nurture them, teach them and discipline them. But never forget that as important as this is, it is a temporary assignment. Your children will grow up and leave home and have lives of their own. On the other hand, your responsibility and commitment to your husband is for a lifetime. Don't make the mistake so many women have of putting all your life and energy into your children to the neglect of your husband. If you do, then when your children leave home, you will have nothing left. The Bible is the best reference I know for showing us the proper balance in family relationships.[69]

There is another subject that is closely related to this that I would like to mention here. It is in regards to pets. It is important to keep your priorities straight and not make pets more important than your husband. If you and your husband like animals and choose to spend time together with your pets, that's one thing, but I have known some women who are so wrapped up in their pets, they have little free time to spend with their husbands.

Here are a few examples. A woman who has horses who spends all of her free time riding them, feeding them and taking care of them. A woman who has a purebred dog and spends all of her free time preparing for and going to dog shows (without her husband). A woman who raises potbellied pigs and spends all of her free time with her potbellied pig "hobby." A woman has so many pets (cats, dogs, birds, fish, etc.) that she has no time left for her husband after she takes care of all her pets. I am sure there are many other examples. These should serve to give you an idea of what I mean when I say don't neglect your husband because you are spending all your free time with your pets.

COMMUNICATION

Communication is the lifeblood of any relationship. Think about it; if you don't communicate, how can you even have a relationship? Open lines of communication are vital to a marriage relationship. Communication is more than what you say. It also includes your tone of voice, your facial expressions, your body language and your behavior. Your words can say one thing while your tone of voice, facial expressions and body language are saying just the opposite. For example, your words can say, "yes, Dear" while your tone of voice, facial expressions and body language are saying, "Oh, all right, but I would really rather not do this at all!"

It is very important for you to learn how to communicate with each other and always be willing to talk things out. If you disagree on something, sit down and talk about it in a calm, adult manner. It is not necessary for you to yell and scream at each other just because you do not see things the same way. Calmly tell your husband how you feel and how you see the situation and encourage him to do the same for you. Try to see things from his point of view and help him to see how you see things. You may still not agree, but at least you will each have the chance to see things from the other one's point of view.

When you are angry it is crucial that you *never* say things that you will regret later. Saying mean, hurtful things to your partner serves no positive purpose. If you feel like saying mean, ugly things, *keep your mouth shut!* Go in another room and shut the door (don't slam it) if you have to, but don't *ever* say mean things in anger. As mentioned earlier in this book, you cannot "take back" something you have said. Verbal attacks are often the "kiss of death" to a marriage relationship. If you were paying attention to the first part of this book then you already know you don't have to say every thing that pops into your head. If it is not going to make your relationship better, just don't say it.

If you do go in another room to "cool off" it is important

that you explain to your spouse that you need to take a break or that you need a "time out." Make sure he understands that it is not about him, it is about you and you need some time to get your thoughts together. This way you won't be "slamming the door" on him emotionally.

There are lessons for us to learn from things that happen in the world around us if we will only see them and apply them to our own lives. The following true story is one such lesson that I would like to share with you.

Last summer there was a major forest fire raging about seven miles from our house. The smoke filled the air for days and some nights; it was hard to go to sleep because the smell of smoke was so strong. They estimated that approximately 4,000 acres were burned.

While the fire was still burning, we drove up to a lake that was about 2 ½ miles from the forest fire. We watched as helicopters scooped up water to help put out the fire. When we left the lake, we drove through the surrounding area to survey the damage. It was devastating! Where once there were beautiful, tall pines and manzanita nothing was left but charred remains and ashes. It was a vast, black scar across the land.

It always saddens me to see such devastation. After something like this, it is never quite the same again. In time the vegetation will grow back and the land will become green again, but the evidence of a large fire will remain for a very long time, and it will never again be like it was.

There is a mountain that we can see from our front windows called "Ash Mountain." The original name was some Indian name, but about fifty years ago a very large forest fire burned over the mountain and all of the big, tall pines were destroyed. A rancher who started a small fire to try to round up some cattle caused the forest fire. He didn't stop to think about what he was doing or the potential damage he might cause. He was thoughtless and careless and the fire got out of hand and caused irreparable damage. Vegetation has grown back over the years, but the tall pines never grew back. The mountain has been changed forever because of one person's thoughtlessness.[70]

The really tragic thing is, just as the carelessness of one man caused irreparable damage to a once beautiful mountain; words said in anger can cause irreparable damage to a once beautiful relationship. Holding your tongue when you are angry can help prevent you from causing a major "forest fire" in your relationship that will change it (in a negative way) forever.

In addition to holding your tongue when you are angry, it is very important to not get physical when you are angry. What I mean by "physical" is never hit each other and don't ever throw things. Hitting and throwing things when you are angry is nothing more than juvenile behavior and not at all an appropriate way for adults to behave.

I want to make another important point here. It takes two people to fight or have an argument. If you refuse to participate, there can be no fight or argument. You can many times diffuse the whole thing by either agreeing with him or simply walking away, and telling your spouse you are calling a "time out." He can't argue or fight all alone. He needs you to participate in order to continue. When you are by yourself, ask yourself, what is my part in this problem? If you can understand how you contribute to the problem, it will help you in solving it. If you do call a "time out" it is important to call a "time in" when you are calmer and better able to deal with the situation in a rational, reasonable manner.

When you are conveying important information to your husband, don't ever assume that your husband understands everything you say or that he even heard what you said. If you have something important to tell your husband, make sure he is not doing something else that will distract him (i.e., watching TV, working on the computer, paying bills, working on the car, playing a video game, has his mind on something else, etc.). If it is that important, make sure you have his undivided attention before you tell him; otherwise your communication may or may not register with him. It is classic for a wife to tell her husband something and later, when it comes up again, the husband says, "I don't remember you telling me that." Don't set yourself up for this to happen to you. Something else you might try when you want to make sure your husband "got the message" is write him a note or even e-mail him and later ask him if he got your note or e-mail and make sure he read and understood it.

If you want further information on communication there are several good resources.[71]

DON'T "LET YOURSELF GO"

The other mistake I have seen wives make is letting themselves go after they get married. I guess they think that they have their "man" now so they don't need to be attractive anymore. Wrong again! Part of having and maintaining a successful, happy relationship is continuing to take care of yourself and look the best that you can. Do I mean you must be a "Stepford Wife"[72] in order to have a happy marriage? Absolutely not! I'm not talking about your makeup being perfect all of the time even after you have changed messy diapers all day and are exhausted from housework. I am also not talking about you looking as perfect and fresh when you come home from a long day at work as you did when you left in the morning. What I am talking about is things like using food for comfort and packing on the pounds; or dressing "frumpy" all of the time because now you are a "mom." Or letting your personal hygiene go to the point that your husband doesn't even want to be near you.

I knew one woman who weighed 130 lbs. and was a size twelve on her wedding day. After eight years of marriage, she weighed 180 lbs. and was wearing size eighteen! The really tragic thing is this woman never had children so she didn't even have that to blame! And no, she wasn't a weight lifter!

> Wedding Day . . .   Two years later.
>
> Don't let yourself go!

Just because you are a mom doesn't mean you can't put on makeup and dress nice for your husband once in a while. Giving birth to children is no excuse to let your body get flabby and out of shape. There are some very simple exercises you can do, starting immediately after you give birth to get your shape back.[73] It will take some work and will power, but the payoff is a happier, more satisfying relationship with your husband.

MAKE THE RELATIONSHIP A PRIORITY

When you are married, the relationship should be more important than either of you individually. Before insisting on having your own way about something, ask yourself if doing so will be good for the relationship. If the answer is "no" then perhaps you should consider backing off about having your own way and put the best interest of the relationship ahead of your personal desires.

When I was growing up and was confronted with particular situations, my mother would often ask me the question, "What difference will it make ten years from now?" Of course, as a child it always irritated me when she would say that. It wasn't until I became an adult that I understood the wisdom behind this question.

It is actually a very good question to ask yourself when you want to do something for yourself that may not be in the best interest of the relationship. Quite often the answer is it won't make very much difference to you personally if you do or don't do a particular thing at a particular time, but it could make a great deal of difference to the relationship ten years later if you keep insisting on having your own way to the detriment of the relationship. If you engage in selfish behavior without regard for your relationship, you may not have a relationship ten years from now!

Every time you put your own personal desires ahead of what is good for the relationship, you are making the statement that you don't really value the relationship all that much. If you make this a habit, over time you will not value the relationship at all and you will have no reason to keep the relationship together.

Let me give you some examples. Say that your husband wants to take you out to dinner one evening and you had planned to do something by yourself that evening that you could do anytime. Which would be better for the relationship, to do something by yourself or to go out with your husband? Will it really make that big of a difference to you personally ten years from now if you postpone what you want to do for yourself to another time so you can spend time with your husband? It could make a difference to the relationship.

Here's another example. Say that you are visiting with another couple and your husband starts telling the other couple about a trip you took. He says you started your trip on a Saturday and you know for sure it was a Sunday. Which would be better for the relationship, to interrupt your husband and embarrass him in front of your friends or to stay quiet and let him continue telling the story?

Again, what difference will it make ten years from now that he was a day off when he told the story to your friends? On the other hand, it could make a very big difference in your relationship if you make a habit of correcting your husband in front of other people.

I am reminded of a quote from a Star Trek movie, "The needs of the many outweigh the needs of the few, or the one." [74] In this case the needs of the relationship outweigh the individual needs of the husband or the wife.

Please do not misunderstand; I am not saying that your personal needs are never important once you get married. The important thing is balance, communication and common sense. Use your head here and just make sure you make the relationship a priority. This applies to your husband as well as you.

The best example that I have ever found of what a healthy husband and wife relationship looks like is in the book of Ephesians in the Bible. The following is from the fifth chapter of Ephesians, New International Version. We will examine these verses one section at a time and I will comment on each section.

Ephesians 5:21-33

"Submit to one another out of reverence for Christ. Wives, submit to your husbands as to the Lord. For the husband is the head of the wife as Christ is the head of the church, his body, of which he is the Savior. Now as the church submits to Christ, so also wives should submit to their husbands in everything."

For some people, this is a very controversial section of the scriptures. It is widely misunderstood by men and women alike, most likely because these verses are often taken out of context.

First of all, let us examine the first sentence. Notice that it says to "submit to one another." This means that there are some ways in which a husband is to submit to his wife as well as a wife submitting to her husband. Quite often this sentence is left out of quotes because husbands are so fond of the following sentences that tell wives to be submissive to their husbands.

Husbands like to then leave out the verses which come after the admonition to wives and go on to tell husbands the proper way to love their wives. Perhaps it is men's propensity for quoting these verses out of context that have caused women's reactionary attitude towards these verses. When put in proper context, I think you will see that when a husband loves his wife in the proper way, and he is willing to submit to her when it is appropriate, she should be willing to submit to him as to the Lord just as the Bible admonishes.

Let us continue and examine what the Bible says about how husbands are to love their wives: "Husbands, love your wives, just as Christ loved the church and gave himself up for her to make her holy, cleansing her by the washing with water through the word, and to present her to himself as a radiant church, without stain or wrinkle or any other blemish, but holy and blameless. In this same way, husbands ought to love their wives as their own bodies. He who loves his wife loves himself. After all, no one ever hated his own body, but he feeds and cares for it, just as Christ does the church—for we are members of his body."

Husbands are given a great responsibility here. The kind of love that is discussed here is the kind of self-sacrificing love that is willing to die for the loved one. This passage also states that a husband ought to love his wife as much as he loves his own body. This is a tall order that takes great commitment and devotion. I am firmly convinced that if more husbands loved their wives in this way, wives would have no problem at all in submitting to their husbands.

This next verse is a familiar quote that is often used in marriage ceremonies: "'For this reason a man will leave his father and mother and be united to his wife, and the two will become one flesh.'"

This is a quote from previous scripture. The reference here is most often interpreted as the sexual union between a husband and wife. I personally believe that this oneness also means being of one mind and one spirit as well as one body. A couple who can achieve this oneness of body, mind and spirit has the best chance of a happy, successful, lifelong relationship.

This last section is sort of the "bottom line" statement that summarizes the verses that go before: "This is a profound mystery—but I am talking about Christ and the church. However, each one of you also must love his wife as he loves himself, and the wife must respect her husband."

Notice the use of "must" here; a husband "*must* love his wife as he loves himself" and "the wife *must* respect her husband." The use of the word "must" here, would suggest that this is not optional. In other words, these two things are a requirement of marriage. If each of you can follow this example, it will go a long way to helping you achieve a happy, lifelong relationship. However, if a man does not intend to love his wife as he loves himself or if a woman does not intend to respect her husband, then it is better not to get married in the first place!

Shakespeare also had some insight into husband and wife

relationships. The following is one of my favorite excerpts from Shakespeare. It is from the play *The Taming of the Shrew*. For those of you who do not know this story, it is the story of a man with two daughters, Katharina and Bianca. It is the custom of that day for the older daughter to marry before the younger daughter. Only problem is, while Bianca has a young man interested in marrying her, Katharina is a willful, obstinate wench and no man wants to have anything to do with her. She is the "Shrew" of the story.

A traveling merchant, Petruchio, comes into town looking for a wife, and since he enjoys a challenge, he takes Katharina to be his wife and proceeds to "tame" her. Most of the play deals with Petruchio's efforts to tame his wife and her resistance to it.

The part I like comes at the end of the play after Katharina has learned a few things about husband-wife relationships. The setting is a social gathering with Petruchio and Katharina in attendance as well as Bianca and her new husband.

The women are gathered together talking and Bianca has a verbal "jousting match" with her new husband and doesn't want to do whatever it is he is requesting of her. This is where Katharina steps in and tells the women how they should behave regarding their husbands.

Since Shakespeare wrote his works over 500 years ago, the language is quite different from the English we speak today. As some people have difficulty understanding fifteenth century English, I have taken the liberty of "translating" the text into modern English to make it easier to understand. The original text appears on the left page and my modern English version appears on the facing page.

While our society has changed considerably since the time this was written, and few wives are supported solely by their husbands, I think the essences of this message still applies today as to the attitude a wife should have toward her husband. This is not unlike what the Bible says about husband-wife relationships. So, read and enjoy!

Shakespeare Version

Fie, fie! unknit that threatening unkind brow,
And dart not scornful glances from those eyes,
To wound thy lord, thy king, thy governor:
It blots thy beauty as frosts do bite the meads,
Confounds thy fame as whirlwinds shake fair buds,
And in no sense is meet or amiable.
A woman moved is like a fountain troubled,
Muddy, ill-seeming, thick, bereft of beauty;
And while it is so, none so dry or thirsty
Will deign to sip or touch one drop of it.
Thy husband is thy lord, thy life, thy keeper,
Thy head, thy sovereign; one that cares for thee,
And for thy maintenance commits his body
To painful labour both by sea and land,
To watch the night in storms, the day in cold,

Modern English Version

Shame on you! Get that ugly scowl off your face,
And stop throwing daggers with your eyes.
When you verbally wound your lord, your king, your governor,
It disfigures your beauty like the frost withers a meadow,
And ruins your reputation like a strong wind shakes flower buds apart.
It is in no way proper or good-natured.
A moody woman is like a murky fountain,
Muddy, dark in appearance, yucky, devoid of beauty,
And while it is like this, not even parched and thirsty men
Will want to take a sip or touch one drop of the water.
Your husband is your lord, your life, your provider,
Your commander-in-chief, and the one who cares for you.
And to take care of you, he commits his body
To painful labor both on the sea and land,
To weather the storms of night and feel the cold of day,

(Shakespeare Version)

Whilst thou liest warm at home, secure and safe;
And craves no other tribute at thy hands
But love, fair looks and true obedience;
Too little payment for so great a debt.
Such duty as the subject owes the prince
Even such a woman oweth to her husband;
And when she is froward, peevish, sullen, sour,
And not obedient to his honest will,
What is she but a foul contending rebel
And graceless traitor to her loving lord?
I am ashamed that women are so simple
To offer war where they should kneel for peace;
Or seek for rule, supremacy and sway,
When they are bound to serve, love and obey.
Why are our bodies soft and weak and smooth,

(Modern English Version)

While you stay warm and cozy at home, safe and secure.
And he desires no other payment from you
But your love, good looks and true obedience.
This is too little payment for so great a debt.
Just as a subject owes payment to a prince, Even so, a woman owes payment to her husband;
And when she is stubbornly willful, irritable, depressing, bad-tempered,
And not obedient to his reasonable desires,
What is she but a disagreeable, disputing rebel,
And one who lacks any sense of what is right or proper and a traitor to her loving lord?
I am ashamed that women are so naïve
To offer war where they should kneel for peace;
Or seek for rule, supremacy and control,
When they have vowed to serve, love and obey.
Why are our bodies soft, and weak and smooth,

(Shakespeare Version)	(Modern English Version)
Unapt to toil and trouble in the world,	Not suitable for hard labor and trouble in the world,
But that our soft conditions and our hearts	But that our temperaments and our hearts
Should well agree with our external parts?	Should be the same as our external parts?
Come, come, you froward and unable worms!	Come now, you stubbornly willful and incompetent, ungrateful wretches!
My mind hath been as big as one of yours,	I used to have an attitude just like yours.
My heart as great, my reason haply more,	I was contrary and even more willful than you.
To bandy word for word and frown for frown;	I matched anyone word for word and frown for frown;
But now I see our lances are but straws,	But now I see we are just full of hot air.
Our strength as weak, our weakness past compare,	We fool ourselves into thinking we are strong when we are weak beyond comparison,
That seeming to be most which we indeed least are.	We try to appear to be the most of what we are the least.
Then vail your stomachs, for it is no boot,	So, stop your bickering and complaining,
And place your hands below your husband's foot:	And place your hands below your husband's foot:
In token of which duty, if he please,	As a symbol of your willingness to submit to him.
My hand is ready; may it do him ease.	I will go first, my hand is ready to demonstrate to my husband and all of you that he is the one who is in charge.

PRAY TOGETHER

In Chapter 8 I discussed the importance of compatibility in the area of spiritual beliefs. One of the best ways you can assure that your marriage relationship lasts a lifetime is to pray together. Statistics show that "couples who pray together stay together."[75] While the U.S. Divorce Statistics for 1997 show that among the general population 50% of first marriages end in divorce and 60% of remarriages end in divorce, recent research by George Barna shows that couples who pray together have reduced their divorce rate to 1%. Praying together was the most significant divorce proofing factor of them all.

According to a 1997 Gallup Poll, the divorce rate among couples who attend church together regularly is 1 out of 2. However, the divorce rate among couples who pray together daily is an astonishing 1 out of 1,152!

My own experience in marriage confirms these statistics. As mentioned earlier, I attended church regularly with two of my ex-husbands and we still ended up getting divorced. However, although we attended church together, we did not pray together very often at all. On the other hand, in my current marriage, my husband and I pray together several times a day, every day. It appears from my own experiences as well as statistics that prayer is the determining factor.

If you would like more information on this subject there are resources available.[76]

DO NICE THINGS FOR EACH OTHER

Just because you get married doesn't mean you can stop doing nice things for each other. Remember all the nice things you did for each other while you were dating? Keep doing those things for the duration of your relationship. As you get to know each other in your married life, be creative and think of ways to please each other and surprise each other in special ways. Let me give you some examples. Every morning my husband fixes a hot cup of herb tea for me. He doesn't have to fix me tea in the morning; it is just a sweet thing he has decided to do for me because he loves me and I appreciate him for it. Sometimes when I know my husband has had an exhausting day, I will rub his feet or his shoulders to help him relax and feel better. He never makes me do this and he seldom even asks for it. I just do it because I love my husband and I want to do nice things for him.

If you have trouble thinking of nice things to do for your husband, just think about what you would do for him if you wanted something special from him. In other words, what would you do for him if you were trying to "butter him up"? Then do those things for him all the time, not just when you want something from him.

Of course, this is a two-way street and it is just as important for your husband to do nice things for you as well. It is much easier to think well of and feel good about someone who is constantly doing nice things for you than it is to think well of and feel good about someone who seldom does anything nice for you. The Bible says we should carry each other's burdens, do good for one another and we should never tire of doing good things. [77] While this is written for Christians in general, it is also good advise for husbands and wives. If you will both adopt the attitude of outdoing each other in doing nice things for the other one, this will go a long way towards making your relationship last a lifetime.

In doing nice things for each other it is important for you to always be thankful and appreciative. In other words, don't take each other for granted. When your husband does something nice for you say, "thank you." Also be sure to tell him often how much you appreciate him and the things he does for you. Besides saying "thank you" and expressing your appreciation for each other, your relationship will be stronger if you often say "I love you" to each other. Say "I love you" in your actions towards each other as well as in your words.

It is also a good idea to thank each other for the things you do on a routine basis. For example, when your husband takes out the trash, tell him, "Thank you for taking out the trash, Honey," or when your husband fixes something around the house, tell him how much you appreciate him doing that. When you do this, be sure it is honest and sincere and *not* condescending. A condescending tone will have the opposite effect.

Of course it is also important for your husband to thank you for the things you do as well, but this book is mainly addressed to you. I hope to write a book later that is addressed to men.

Another aspect of being thankful and appreciative is showing gratitude for gifts you are given by your spouse. Husbands don't always know the right things to buy for their wives, but as I'm sure you have heard somewhere before, "it's the thought that counts." This really is true so be sure not to discourage your husband from buying you gifts by finding fault with the gift.

Let me give you an example of what I mean here. I knew a professional couple who had been married for several years. The husband often told me how he could never seem to please his wife with the gifts that he bought for her. The wife's side of the story was that her husband was always buying things for her (usually clothes) that were the wrong size or the wrong color and she would always have to take them back and exchange them.

The husband finally decided that since he seemed to be such a failure at buying the right clothes for his wife, he would buy her something else that was sure to please her. He told me of how he planned to buy her an expensive, genuine, pearl necklace. The next time I saw the wife, she told me how her husband had bought her a genuine, pearl necklace, but she was quick to point out to him how the pearls in the necklace were oval and did not match her round, pearl earrings. She immediately asked him where he had purchased the necklace so she could take it back and exchange it for one that matched her earrings! When she told me this, I could not believe her nonchalant attitude and apparent lack of awareness regarding her husband's feelings. It would have been much better for her to show her husband appreciation for the pearl necklace and then later purchase oval, pearl earrings to match if she really thinks she can't wear "round" pearl earrings with an "oval" pearl necklace.

The point here is, no matter what your husband buys for you, appreciate the gift. Even if it is not something you are thrilled about, never make an issue of that fact. Be appreciative of the gift and the fact that he was thinking of you and if you absolutely have to return it for exchange, don't make a big deal about it.

If your husband enjoys buying clothes for you, one way to avoid the "wrong color" or "wrong size" scenario is to suggest that he take you with him when he buys clothes for you. Shopping together will not only assure that you end up with clothes that you like and he likes seeing on you, it will also strengthen your relationship.

Here are some more ways you can do nice things for each other. Someone sent me a sweet story about a couple who played a game with each other called "SHMILY." [78] I was so taken with this story that my husband and I have started playing this game as well. We have a lot of fun with it and it is a reminder to both of us that we are still very much in love with each other. My husband even made a custom coffee (tea) mug for me that says, "SHMILY, If necessary, I would travel through time to be with you."

You can also do nice things for each other when you are around other people. Whenever my husband and I get together socially with another couple, we are sure to include in our conversation stories from our life together that illustrate how much we appreciate each other. Sometimes we talk about how we met and what we liked about each other at first. We sometimes talk about the nice things we have done for each other or the fun trips we have taken together. In essence, we tell them our "love story" which for us is still being written. We also encourage the other couple to tell us what they appreciate about each other and have them tell us their "love story."

It is amazing how good it makes you feel and how much closer you are to your spouse when you hear him/her telling other people what he/she likes most about you or why he/she appreciates you. When you are around other people, it is much better for your relationship if you will build each other up and say nice things about each other rather than argue or pick at each other and tear each other down.

If you stop doing nice things for each other, it tends to start this "chain reaction." You don't do nice things for each other so you stop feeling as close as you once did and because you don't feel as close as you once did you don't feel like doing nice things for each other. It reminds me of the song, "You don't bring me flowers anymore" sung by Neil Diamond and Barbara Streisand. [79] If you are not familiar with this song, it is a song about how love has grown cold and a couple has grown apart. If you don't want this to happen to you, be sure to keep doing nice things for each other.

What works for me and my husband is, as much as possible, I take care of his needs and as much as possible, he takes care of my needs. That way we are both taken care of without each of us being selfish.

One of the things that sometimes keeps a couple from doing nice things for each other is arguments, disagreements or outright fights. When you live with another person day in and day out, it is impossible for you to agree on everything all the time. Just because you have a disagreement doesn't mean you should stop doing nice things for each other. In fact, if you can be big enough to do nice things for each other even when you don't agree, it will help you to deal with the disagreement better and help you to reconcile your differences.

FINANCES

The area of finance has the potential for causing marital discord. It is important that you come to some agreements on how your family finances will be handled. No matter which one of you takes care of paying the bills and other financial matters, it is important for the other person to be aware of what is going on and what your financial picture looks like at any given time. That way, if something happens where the one who has been paying the bills and taking care of other financial matters cannot do so, the other person will not be totally in the dark and at a loss as to what needs to be paid and when.

It is also a good idea to come to an agreement about how much either of you can spend without first consulting with the other. For some couples that amount could be $100 or you could agree for it to be $500. If you are on a very limited budget, it could be a much lower amount. Whatever the amount is you agree on, never spend more than that without consulting your partner first. As your financial picture changes, be sure to adjust the amount you can spend accordingly.

Another suggestion is to have a financial "summit" at least once a week to discuss what is going on with your family finances so both of you will be well aware of your financial picture.

JEALOUSY

Since we are talking about how to make a marriage last a lifetime, I think it is important to talk about jealousy. There are two meanings of the word "jealousy" I would like to address here.

First of all, it is very important that neither of you become jealous of the other for any reason. For example, if your husband gets recognition for something that leaves you in the shadows, don't be jealous of him. If you really love him, you should be happy for him that he is being recognized. I refer you back to Chapter 2 and the definition of "love." It is also important for your husband not to become jealous of you in this way.

The second kind of jealousy is the kind we hear about in songs and see in the movies. It is where a husband becomes jealous because he sees his wife talking to another man or where a wife becomes jealous because she sees her husband looking at another woman. There is no place for this kind of jealousy in a happy, healthy marriage. A marriage relationship is based on trust. If you love each other and trust each other then you won't be suspicious and jealous of every person of the opposite sex who comes in contact with your mate. It is also important to trust yourself that no matter what happens in your relationship, you will be okay and you will survive. If you trust yourself in this way you will realize that it is juvenile to be jealous.

One other thing while we are on this subject. Whether men are married or not, it is normal and natural for them to notice attractive women. Just because you see your husband looking at another woman, that does not mean he doesn't love you or he would rather be with her. It just means he is a normal, healthy man who is noticing an attractive woman. If you get mad at him for looking at other women you will only put a barrier between you.

I knew of one husband who went on a trip with his wife to a tropical island where there was an abundance of bikini-clad "babes." Every time she caught him looking at another woman, she punched him. He came home from this trip with a multitude of bruises. There is no need for this kind of behavior. Just accept the fact that men like to look at attractive women and don't see it as a threat to your relationship. Acting jealous and giving your husband a bad time about looking at other women is just a sign of your own insecurity.

While doing research for this work, I have come across many lists of suggestions for a happy marriage. To summarize this chapter, I would like to present the following compilation of the various lists (authors unknown). Some of these ideas are presented in the text of this book, while others are new. I present the following list to you for your consideration.

Practical Tips to Husbands and Wives for a Happy Marriage

To Wives:

1. On special occasions dress up for your husband as you did before marriage.
2. Don't expect him to apologize even when he is wrong. Let it pass.
   Assure him he is the greatest man alive.
3. Do not nag. It never gets the results you want and it only irritates your husband.
4. Don't hit your husband over the head with faith, the Bible or God.
   Remember the Word of God is a sword not a hammer.
5. Don't ever tell him you made a big sacrifice when you married him. Women are helpers, not competitors.

To Husbands and Wives:

6. Remember the happy hours of early love.
7. Honor the sanctity of marriage.
8. Greet each other affectionately every time you meet.
9. At least once in every day, say one kind or complimentary thing to your life's partner.

10. When you have done something wrong, admit it and ask for forgiveness.
11. Practice forgiveness.
12. Spend less than you make, be responsible with money, and (as much as possible) stay out of debt.
13. Rejoice in every moment that God has given you together, no matter what your financial circumstances are.
14. Never taunt with mistakes of the past.
15. If you feel you must criticize do so lovingly.
16. Never both be angry at the same time.
17. Never yell at each other unless the house is on fire.
18. Remember, it takes two to make a quarrel.
19. Never go to sleep with a quarrel unsettled.
20. Yield to the wishes of the other as an exercise in self-discipline, if you can't think of a better reason.
21. Never make a remark at the expense of each other.
22. If you have a choice between making yourself or your spouse look good, choose your spouse
23. Neglect the whole world rather than each other

Chapter 11

Keeping The Romance Alive

Quite often it is all too easy to let the romance slip away once you are married. This is especially true if and when you have children. While statistics show time and again that over time most couples let the romance die in their relationship, this need not be the case for you. There are many things you can do to keep romance a part of your relationship in spite of children, jobs, stress and difficult times.

Here are some examples and suggestions. I know one couple who made it a rule (once they had children) to hire a babysitter and go out on a "date" with each other once a week. No matter how busy their schedules were or how demanding the children became at times, they faithfully kept their date with each other every week. One day out of every seven was theirs and theirs alone. This was their time to spend together building their relationship.

This same couple would also plan a weekend getaway at least once a year on their anniversary. I am happy to report that this couple has been happily married now for over twenty-five years. They have raised three wonderful children. This husband and wife are two of the happiest people I have ever known and even after twenty-five years together, they still behave like newlyweds.

If your husband likes to see you in lingerie, one of the things you can do to keep the romance alive is to wear it for him on a regular basis. By "regular basis" I don't mean every time you are together sexually, but I do mean more than just a few times a year. Find out what kind of lingerie your husband thinks is sexy and buy a few outfits and wear them.

Wear lingerie for your husband!

Not all husbands would enjoy doing this, but perhaps your husband would be willing to take you shopping for lingerie. That way he can pick the outfits he wants you to try on and buy the ones he likes best. You may not need lingerie to get you in the "mood" but if he likes you to wear it, then I would suggest you do so for him.

If your husband doesn't want to take you shopping for lingerie, but he would like for you to buy it to wear, sit down with him and look at some lingerie catalogs together and get an idea of what kind of lingerie he thinks is sexy. If you don't know where to find lingerie catalogs, I suggest you do a search on the internet on "lingerie." You may be surprised at how many resources you find.

Another thing you can do is tell your husband the kinds of things that put you in the "mood" for love and encourage him to do those things for you. For most men, if he finds out he will get what he wants by doing what you want, trust me, he will do what you want. One word of caution here; once you tell him the things that put you in the "mood," be sure to follow through and be in the "mood" when he does any of those things for you. If what you have told him stops working, you can be sure he will stop doing those things for you. This is just human nature.

Find out what your husband's favorite foods are and fix them often. If you don't know how to cook what he likes best, learn how. You may not even like to cook, but even if you never cook anything else, learn how to cook two or three of his favorite dishes. Cooking what a man likes to eat is one way to keep the romance alive.

Tell your husband what a good lover he is. Men never get tired of hearing this. If you don't think he's a good lover then help him to learn.[80]

In the section about sexual compatibility, I said I would say more later about it not being fair to your boyfriend to use sex to get him to commit to you and then leave him in the cold. Well, now that we are talking about what it takes to make a marriage last a lifetime, this is the time and the place to be more specific.

Sex is a very important part of a marriage relationship. Some people feel uncomfortable talking about sex, but since it is so important, I feel I must talk about it. In my dealings with people as a therapist, I could not believe how many times husbands would confide to me that when they were first married their wives were more than happy to fulfill their sexual needs. However, after a few years of marriage, their wives turned cold sexually and no longer seemed to be interested in sex at all.

One husband told me that after eight years of marriage, his wife would no longer let him even sleep in the same bed with her. They had separate bedrooms and only had sex with each other about every six months or so.

> Not tonight Dear, I have a headache!

Don't turn cold after a few years!

The most common sexual complaint I got from husbands was that their wives refused to give them oral sex. No matter how you may personally feel about oral sex, it is important for you to understand that most men really like it. If you refuse to do this for your husband, it could be quite detrimental to your marriage.

I fully understand that women are wired differently than men and most of the time sex is not the first thing on their minds. However, if you want to have a happy, lifelong relationship, it will be a good idea if you do whatever you have to do to stay interested in sex[81] and make sure you do your best to meet your husband's needs in this area. I suggest you read what the Bible says about the place that sex has in marriage,[82] you might be surprised.

Find ways to make your sexual encounters fun. If you have fun with sex, you are more likely to enjoy your intimate times together. Sex need not be "routine" or "boring." Use your imagination and keep the "spark" alive in your sex life. Most husbands want their wives to act like genteel ladies in public and like ladies of the evening in the bedroom. This may be a difficult concept for you to grasp, but it is nonetheless how most men think. Ask your husband if he agrees with this idea. There is a very high probability that he will.

It is simply not fair for you to slack off in meeting your husband's sexual needs and expect him to remain faithful to you. Men are only human and even the best of them can be tempted if they aren't getting their sexual needs met at home.

Another suggestion for keeping the romance alive is to do romantic things with each other. Find out what activities each of you thinks is romantic and plan to do those things. It's okay to use your imagination and be creative. Here are a few suggestions based on what other people think is romantic.

- Write love poems to each other.
- Write love letters to each other.
- Listen to romantic music together.
- Have dinner by candle light.
- Take a walk together holding hands.
- Have a picnic in the park or in the country.
- Take a moonlit stroll on the beach.
- Watch the sunset together.
- Watch the sunrise together.
- Give romantic cards to each other.
- Buy little gifts for each other when there is no special occasion.

A rule of thumb here is to remember the kinds of things that made you fall in love with each other in the first place, and keep doing those things throughout your married life.

If you keep "courting" each other, chances are very good that you will stay together for a lifetime.

CONCLUSION

As I mentioned earlier, this is not meant to be a rulebook. This book is also not a guarantee for love and happiness. What I have done here is share with you from my experience and offer you guidelines that I hope will help you towards making better choices in your life and allow you to have the happiest life possible for you. If you have any questions or comments about this book, please contact me. I would love to hear from you. [83]

Reference Guide

[1] Appendix 4, E
[2] Appendix 2, A
[3] Appendix 1, D
[4] Appendix 4, E
[5] Appendix 1, D
[6] Appendix 4, E
[7] Appendix 3, A
[8] Appendix 3, B
[9] Appendix 1, C
[10] Appendix 1, I, Appendix 4, I
[11] Appendix 4, G
[12] Appendix 3, C
[13] Appendix 4, C
[14] Appendix 4, F
[15] Appendix 1, D and G
[16] Appendix 4, K-1 and K-4
[17] Appendix 4, K-2
[18] Appendix 4, L
[19] Appendix 1, D
[20] Appendix 2, B
[21] Appendix 1, D
[22] Appendix 5, A
[23] Appendix 3, D
[24] Appendix 3, E
[25] Appendix 5, A
[26] Appendix 5, B
[27] Appendix 5, C
[28] Appendix 1, D
[29] Appendix 4, K-3
[30] Appendix 5, A
[31] Appendix 5, D
[32] Appendix 2, C
[33] Appendix 2, D
[34] Appendix 5, A
[35] Appendix 5, E
[36] Appendix 3, F
[37] Appendix 2, E
[38] Appendix 3, G
[39] Appendix 1, A
[40] Appendix 3, H
[41] Appendix 1, A
[42] Appendix 3, I
[43] Appendix 3, J
[44] Appendix 1, A
[45] Appendix 2, F
[46] Appendix 5, A
[47] Appendix 5, F
[48] Appendix 1, D, Appendix 2, G
[49] Appendix 1, D
[50] Appendix 5, A

[51] Appendix 2, H
[52] Appendix 5, A
[53] Appendix 1, H
[54] Appendix 5, G
[55] Appendix 5, H
[56] Appendix 5, I
[57] Appendix 5, J
[58] Appendix 5, K
[59] Appendix 5, L
[60] Appendix 1, E
[61] Appendix 2, I
[62] Appendix 5, M
[63] Appendix 5, N
[64] Appendix 1, D
[65] Appendix 5, A
[66] Appendix 5, O
[67] Appendix 4, M
[68] Appendix 5, A
[69] Appendix 2, J
[70] Appendix 5, P
[71] Appendix 1, D
[72] Appendix 5, Q
[73] Appendix 3, K
[74] Appendix 5, R
[75] Appendix 5, A
[76] Appendix 1,A
[77] Appendix 2, K
[78] Appendix 5, S
[79] Appendix 5, T
[80] Appendix 1, F
[81] Appendix 4, N, Appendix 1, F
[82] Appendix 2, L
[83] Appendix 4, J

Appendix 1

Recommended Books, Audio Tapes and Video Tapes

A) Christian Faith

Books by C.S. Lewis:

All My Road Before Me: the Diary of C. S. Lewis, 1922-1927
San Diego: Harcourt Brace Jovanovich, 1991. Walter Hooper, ed.

Beyond Personality: the Christian Idea of God
London: Geoffrey Bless, 1944.

Christian Reflections
A collection of papers William B. Eerdmans, 1967
Chronicles of Narni" (A Collection of seven books)
New York: Collier Books, 1970.

The Four Loves
London: Geoffrey Bles, 1958.

God in the Dock: Essays on Theology and Ethics
Ed. Walter Hooper. Grand Rapids, MI: Eerdmans, 1970.

The Great Divorce
London: Geoffrey Bles, 1946; rpt. New York: Macmillan, 1977.

Mere Christianity
New York: MacMillian, 1943.

Miracles: A Preliminary Study
London: Geoffrey Bles, 1947.

The Problem of Pain
London: Geoffrey Bles, 1940.

Reflections on the Psalms
London: Geoffrey Bles, 1958.

The Screwtape Letters
London: Geoffrey Bles, 1942; rpt., with "Screwtape Proposes a Toast" and a new Preface. New York: Macmillan, 1962.

The Weight of Glory
MacMillian, 1980

The World's Last Night
San Diego: Harcourt Brace Jovanovich, 1973

Books by Dr. Hugh Ross:

The Genesis Question
Publisher: NavPress Publishing Group, October 1998, ISBN: 1576831116

Beyond the Cosmos
Publisher: NavPress Publishing Group, January 1999, ISBN: 1576831124

Creation and Time
Publisher: NavPress Publishing Group, March 1994,
ISBN: 0891097767

The Creator and the Cosmos
Third Expanded Edition
Publisher: NavPress Publishing Group, June 2001
ISBN: 1576832880

The Fingerprint of God
Publisher: Whitaker House, July 2000
ISBN: 0883686279

Books by Richard Wurmbrand:

In the Face of Surrender
Publisher: Bridge-Logos Publishers, June 1998
ISBN: 0882707558

In God's Underground
Publisher: Living Sacrifice Book Company, June 1993,
ISBN: 0882640038

From Suffering to Triumph
Publisher: Kregel Publications, April 1993
ISBN: 0825440610

Christ on the Jewish Road
Publisher: Living Sacrifice Book Company, September 1993,

Sweetest Song
Publisher: Living Sacrifice Book Company, April 1993,
ISBN: 0551016523

Books and Audiotapes by Dr. Leonard G. Horowitz:
(1-888-508-4787)

Complete Jewish Bible
(For Christians)
Publisher: Tetrahedron Publishing Group

End Times: Preparedness, Prophecy and Propaganda (90-Minute Audio)
Publisher: Tetrahedron Publishing Group

Why It's Time Jews and Christians Unite
(3-Hour Audio)
Publisher: Tetrahedron Publishing Group

Books by various authors:

The Pastor's Wife
Authors: Sabina Wurmbrand, Charles Foley
Publisher: Living Sacrifice Book Company, January 1989

I'm More Than The Pastor's Wife
Author: Lorna Dobson
Publisher: Zondervan Publishing House, May 1995,
ISBN: 0310485517

Christianity Unmasqued
Author: Dan Israel
S O S Press, Limited, April 1999

Corrie Ten Boom: Her Story: A Collection Consisting of the Hiding Place, Tramp for the Lord, and Jesus Is Victor
Author: Corrie Ten Boom
Publisher: BBS Publishing Corporation, September 1995,
ISBN: 0884861260

Books on Prayer in Marriage:

Moments Together for Couples
Authors: Dennis Rainey and Barbara Rainey

Publisher: Gospel Light Publications, July 1998
ISBN: 0830717544

Becoming Soul Mates
Authors: Les Parrott III and Leslie Parrott
Publisher: Zondervan Publishing House, November 1997,
ISBN: 0310219264

When Couples Pray: The Little-Known Secret to Lifelong Happiness in Marriage
Author: Cheri Fuller
Publisher: Multnomah Publishers, Inc., January 2001,
ISBN: 1576736660

Prayer Can Change Your Marriage
Author: Ron Auch
Publisher: New Leaf Press, Inc., April 2001
ISBN: 0892211180

What Happens When Husbands and Wives Pray Together
Authors: Carey Moore and Pamela Rosewell Moore
Publisher: Revell, Fleming H. Company, March 1999,
ISBN: 0800786599

B) Health Education

Books and Tapes from the "Reality Zone":
(*http://www.realityzone.com/healnut.html*)

Alternative Medicine: *The Definitive Guide*
Compiler: Burton Goldberg Group
Publisher: Future Medicine Publishing, Inc., September 1998,
ISBN: 1887299335

Alternative Medicine's Guide to Cancer

Authors: W. John Diamond, Burton Goldberg, W. Lee Cowden
Publisher: Future Medicine Publishing, Inc., April 1997, ISBN: 1887299017

Alive and Well: One Doctor's Experience with Nutrition in the Treatment of Cancer Patients
Author: Philip E. Binzel Jr., M.D.
Publisher: American Media, October 1994
ISBN: 0912986174

Cancer: Cause, Cure and Cover-up
Author: Ron Gdanski
Publisher: New Century Press, January 2000
ISBN: 0968566502

Cancer Diagnosis: What to Do Next
Authors: J. John Diamond, Burton Goldberg, W. Lee Cowden
Publisher: AlternativeMedicine.com Books, June 2000, ISBN: 1887299408

Cancer Therapy
Author: Ralph Moss Ph.D.
Publisher: Equinox Press, March 1993
ISBN: 1881025063

Cross Currents: The Perils of Electropollution, The Promise of Electromedicine
Author: Robert O. Becker
Publisher: The Putnam Publishing Group, January 1991, ISBN: 0874776090

Genetically Engineered Food: Changing the Nature of Nature
Authors: Martin Teitel, Kimberly A. Wilson
Publisher: Inner Traditions International, Limited, November 1999, ISBN: 0892818883

Alternative Medicine Guide to Heart Disease, Stroke and High Blood Pressure
Authors: Burton Goldberg, Alternative Medicine Digest Staff
Publisher: Future Medicine Publishing, Inc., February 1998,
ISBN: 1887299270

Hoxsey: The Quack Who Cured Cancer?
(96 Minute Video)

Hoxsey—When Healing Becomes A Crime
Authors: Kenny Ausubel, Ken Ausubel
Publisher: Inner Traditions International, Limited, April 2000,
ISBN: 0892819251

It's All In Your Head: The Link between Mercury Amalgams and Illness
Author: Hal A. Huggens
Publisher: Avery Publishing Group, Inc., August 1993,
ISBN: 0895295504

Sharks Don't Get Cancer: How Sharks Cartilage Could Save Your Life
Authors: I. William Lane With Linda Comac
Publisher: Avery Publishing Group, Inc., August 1992,
ISBN: 0895295202

Vaccination: The Hidden Truth
(1 ½ Hour Video)

World Without AIDS
Authors: Leon Chaitow, Simon Martin
Publisher: Thorsons, September 1988
ISBN: 0722516320

World Without Cancer: The Story of Vitamin B17
American Media (Editor) Forward by G. Edward Griffin
Publisher: American Media, December 1996
ISBN: 0912986190

Books, Audiotapes and Videos by Dr. Leonard G. Horowitz:
(1-888-508-4787)

Emerging Viruses: Aids and Ebola
(Book, 3-Hour Audio and 2 ½ Hour Video)
Publisher: Tetrahedron Publishing Group

Healing Codes for the Biological Apocalypse
(Book, 4-Hour Audio & 4 Hour Video)
Publisher: Tetrahedron Publishing Group

Death in the Air: Globalism, Terrorism & Toxic Warfare
Publisher: Tetrahedron Publishing Group

Gulf War Syndrome: The Spreading Epidemic Cover-up (3 ½-Hour Video)
Publisher: Tetrahedron Publishing Group

The Nazi-American Biomedical/Biowarfare Connection (3-Hour Audio)
Publisher: Tetrahedron Publishing Group

Virus Makers of the CIA
(3-Hour Audio)
Publisher: Tetrahedron Publishing Group

Deadly Innocence: The Kimberly Bergalis Case (3-Hour Audio, 2 ½-Hour Video & Paperback Book)
Publisher: Tetrahedron Publishing Group

C) Health & Nutrition

Books from the "Reality Zone":
(*http://www.realityzone.com/healnut.html*)

Allergy Free

Authors: Konrad Kail with Burton Goldberg & Bobbi Lawrence
Publisher: AlternativeMedicine.com Books, August 2000,
ISBN: 188729936X

Beating Cancer with Nutrition
Authors: Dr. Patrick Quillin with Noreen Quillin
ublisher: Nutrition Times Press, Incorporated, January 2001,
ISBN: 0963837281

The Chelation Way
Author: Dr. Morton Walker
Publisher: Avery Publishing Group, Inc., October 1989,
ISBN: 089529415X

Dealing with Depression Naturally: Alternative and Complementary Therapies for Restoring Emotional Health
Author: Syd Baumel
Publisher: McGraw-Hill Trade, May 2000
ISBN: 0658002910

DMSO Nature's Healer
Author: Dr. Morton Walker
Publisher: Avery Publishing Group, Inc., December 1996,
ISBN: 0895295482

Encyclopedia of Nutritional Supplements
Author: Michael T. Murray, N.D.
Publisher: Prima Health Publishing, Inc., July 1996,
ISBN: 0761504109

The Enzyme Cure
Authors: Lita Lee, Alternative Medicine Digest, Lisa Turner
Publisher: Future Medicine Publishing, Inc., March 1998,
ISBN: 188729922X

Grow Young with Hgh

Authors: Ronald Klatz & Carol Kahn
Publisher: Harper Trade, April 1998
ISBN: 0060984341

Natural Health Secrets from Around the World
Glenn W. Geelhoed (Editor)
Publisher: Keats Publishing, Inc., September 1997
ISBN: 0879838051

Psoriasis Cure
Author: Lisa LeVan
Publisher: Penguin USA, May 1999
ISBN: 0895299178

The Skin Cancer Answer
Authors: W. William Lane & Linda Comac
Publisher: Avery Publishing Group, Inc., January 1999,
ISBN: 0895298651

Third Opinion: An International Directory to Alternative Therapy Centers for the Treatment and Prevention of Cancer and Other Degenerative Diseases
Author: John M. Fink
Publisher: Avery Publishing Group, Inc., April 1997,
ISBN: 0895297701

Books, Audiotapes, & Videos by Dr. Leonard G. Horowitz:
(1-888-508-4787)

Taking Care of Yourself: Boosting Immunity
(9-Hour Audio with Workbook)
Publisher: Tetrahedron Publishing Group

Horowitz 'On Vaccines'
(90-Minute Audio)
Publisher: Tetrahedron Publishing Group

Horowitz 'On Healing'
(90-Minute Audio)
Publisher: Tetrahedron Publishing Group

Nutritional Supplements for Immunity, Energy, Acuity and more
(3-Hour Audio)
Publisher: Tetrahedron Publishing Group

Healing Celebrations
(Book and 8-Hour Audio)
Publisher: Tetrahedron Publishing Group

Freedom from Headaches and TMJ Pain Syndrome (90-Minute Audio and Guidebook)
Publisher: Tetrahedron Publishing Group

Freedom from Teeth Clenching and Night Grinding (60-Minute Audio and Guidebook)
Publisher: Tetrahedron Publishing Group

Freedom from Desk Job Stress and Computer Strain (90-Minute Audio and Guidebook)
Publisher: Tetrahedron Publishing Group

Freedom from Dental Anxiety
(3-Hour Audio and Guidebook)
Publisher: Tetrahedron Publishing Group

D) Personal Self-help

Positive Affirmations

What to Say When You Talk to Yourself
Author: Shad Helmstetter, Ph.D.
Publisher: Grindle Press, June 1986

ISBN: 0937065056

The Game of Life Affirmation and Inspiration Cards: Positive Words for a Positive Life
Author: Florence Scovel Shinn Adapted by Marie Haddad
Publisher: DeVorss & Company, December 1997
ISBN: 0875166172

Soul Talk: Positive Mind Treatments to Turn Your Life Around
Author: Hubert Pryor
Publisher: Crossroad Publishing Company, November 1995,
ISBN: 0824515234

Life Scripts: How to "Talk" to Yourself for Positive Results
Author: Ursula Markham
Publisher: Element Books, March 1994
ISBN: 1852304324

Assertiveness

Asserting Yourself
Authors: Sharon Anthony Bower & Gordon H. Bower
Publisher Perseus Books, 1991
ISBN: 0201570882

Asserting Your Self: How to Feel Confident about Getting More from Life
Author: Cathy Birch
Publisher: How to Books, June 2000
ISBN: 1857034333

How to Say No without Feeling Guilty: And Say Yes to More Time and More Joy
Authors: Patti Breitman & Connie Hatch
Publisher: Broadway Books, April 2001
ISBN: 0767903803

Personal Responsibility

Taking Responsibility: Self-Reliance and the Accountable Life
Author: Nathaniel Branden Ph.D.
Publisher: Simon and Schuster Trade, March 1997
ISBN: 0684832488

Grow up! How Taking Responsibility Can Make You a Happy Adult
Author: Frank Pittman
Publisher: St. Martin's Press, Inc., June 1999
ISBN: 1582380406

Diplomacy

How to Handle Disagreeable Situations in an Agreeable Manner
Authors: Heather Latimer & Kate Greenaway (Illustrator)
Publisher: Papyrus & Letterbox of London, January 2000,
ISBN: 0943698235

Speaking Your Mind in 101 Difficult Situations
Author: Don Gabor
Publisher: Simon & Schuster Trade, March 1994
ISBN: 0671795058

Self-Esteem

The Woman's Guide to Total Self-Esteem: The Eight Secrets You Need to Know
Authors: Stephanie Dillon, Ph.D. & M. Christina Benson, M.D.
Publisher: New Harbinger Publications, June 2001,
ISBN: 1572242418

The Secret of the Shadow: The Power of Owning Your Whole Story
Author: Debbie Ford
Publisher: Harper San Francisco, December 2001,
ISBN: 0062517821

The Power of Self-Esteem
Author: Nathaniel Branden
Publisher: Health Communications, Inc., January 1992,
ISBN: 1558742131

"Life's Too Short: Pull the Plug on Self-Defeating Behavior and Turn on the Power of Self-Esteem
Author: Abraham J. Twerski
Publisher: St. Martin's Press, Inc., April 1997
ISBN: 0312155700

Ten Days to Self-Esteem, Vol. 1
Author: David D. Burns, M.D.
Publisher: William Morrow & Co, September 1993,
ISBN: 0688094554

Recognizing Strengths

Now, Discover Your Strengths
Authors: Marcus Buckingham and Donald O. Clifton
Publisher: The Free Press, January 2001
ISBN: 0743201140

The Self-Esteem Companion: Simple Excercises to Help You Challenge Your Inner Critic and Celebrate Your Personal Strengths
Authors: Matthew McKay, Patrick Fanning, Carole Honeychurch and Catharine Sutker
Publisher: New Harbinger Publications, June 1999
ISBN: 1572241381

I Didn't Place in the Talent Race, but . . . : A Woman's Guide to Recognizing Her Strengths
Author: Anya Bateman
Publisher: Deseret Book Company, May 1993
ISBN: 0875793541

Security and Adequacy

The Tender Heart: Conquering Your Insecurity
Author: Joseph Nowinski, Ph.D.
Publisher: Simon and Schuster Trade, April 2001
ISBN: 068487167X

101 Ways to Overcome Insecurity
Author: Marilyn Hickey
Publisher: Marilyn Hickey Ministries, July 1998
ISBN: 1564411753

Psycho-Cybernetics
Author: Maxwell Maltz, M.D.
Publisher: Simon and Schuster Trade, March 1970
ISBN: 0671700758

Love Yourself, Heal Your Life Workbook
Author: Louise L. Hay
Publisher: Hay House, Inc., May 1990
ISBN: 0937611697

Positive Mental Attitude

The Power of Positive Thinking
Author: Norman Vincent Peal
Publisher: Random House, Incorporated, July 1996,
ISBN: 0449911470

Success Through a Positive Mental Attitude
Author: Napolean Hill with W. Clement Stone
Publisher: Simon and Schuster Trade, November 1976,
ISBN: 0671743228

As a Man Thinketh
Author: James Allen

Publisher: DeVorss and Company, August 1975
ISBN: 087516000X

Attitude Is Everything: 10 Life-Changing Steps to Turning Attitude into Action
Author: Keith Harrell
Publisher: Harper Trade, March 2000
ISBN: 006019605X

Personality Types

What Type Am I? Discover Who You Really Are
Author: Renee Baron
Publisher: Viking Penguin, July 1998
ISBN: 014026941X

Personality Types
Don Richard Riso with Russ Hudson
Publisher: Houghton Mifflin Company, August 1996,
ISBN: 0395798671

Gifts Differing: Understanding Personality Type
Authors: Isabel Briggs Myers with Peter B. Myers
Publisher: Consulting Psychologists Press, Inc., May 1995,
ISBN: 089106074X

Communication

Will the Real Me Please Stand up? 25 Guidelines for Good Communication
Authors: John Powell, Loretta Brady
Publisher: Resources for Christian Living, April 1990,
ISBN: 088347316X

How to Have Confidence And Power In Dealing With People
Author: Les Giblin
Publisher: Prentice Hall PTR, February 1986

ISBN: 0134106717

How To Win Friends and Influence People (Revised Edition)
Author: Dale Carnegie
Publisher: Simon and Schuster Trade, June 1982
ISBN: 0671723650

Body Language
Author: Julius Fast
Publisher: Fine Communications, September 1992,
ISBN: 1567310044

Getting What You Want: How to Reach Agreement and Resolve Conflict Every Time
Author: Kare Anderson
Publisher: the Penguin Group, January 1994
ISBN: 0452270537

E) Racial Differences

Marriage Across the Color Line
Editor: Clotye M. Larsson
Publisher: Johnson Publishing Company, Inc., January 1965,
ISBN: 0874850142

Love's Revolution: Racial Intermarriage
Author: Maria P. Root
Publisher: Temple University Press, February 2001,
ISBN: 1566398266

Interracial Intimacy: The Regulation of Race and Romance
Author: Rachel F. Moran
Publisher: University of Chicago Press, May 2001
ISBN: 0226536629

F) Sex and Intimacy

The Power of Unconditional Love: 21 Guidelines for Beginning, Improving, and Changing Your Most Meaningful Relationships (Rev. 4th ed)
Authors: Ken Keyes With Penny Keyes
Publisher: Love Line Books, April 1990
ISBN: 0915972190

Five Steps to Romantic Love: A Workbook for Readers of Love Busters and His Needs, Her Needs
Author: Willard F. Harley
Publisher: Fleming H. Revell, Company, April 1997,
ISBN: 0800756231

Hot Monogamy: Essential Steps to More Passionate, Intimate Lovemaking
Authors: Patricia Love and Jo Robinson
Publisher: Penguin USA, December 1994
ISBN: 0452273668

Expanded Orgasm: Soar to Ecstasy at Your Lover's Every Touch
Author: Patricia Taylor
Publisher: Sourcebooks, Incorporated, November 2001,
ISBN: 1570718318

How to Be Your Husband's Best Friend: 365 Ways to Express Your Love
Authors: Cay Bolin and Cindy Trent
Publisher: Pinon Press, December 1994
ISBN: 0891098747

Complete Guide to Sex after Marriage
Author: Phil Goode
Publisher: CCC Publications, May 1999
ISBN: 1576440923

G) Success and Motivation

The 7 Habits of Highly Effective People
Author: Stephen R. Covey
Publisher: Simon and Schuster Trade, August 1990
ISBN: 0671708635

The Wisdom of Florence Scovel Shinn
Author: Florence Scovel Shinn
Publisher: Simon and Schuster Trade, May 1989
ISBN: 0671682288

The Gift of Acabar
Author: Og Mandino and Buddy Kaye
Publisher: Bantam Books Inc., May 1979
ISBN: 0553260847

Say Yes to Your Potential
Author: Skip Ross with Carole C. Carlson
Publisher: W Publishing Group, May 1985
ISBN: 0849930146

The Magic of Thinking Big
Author: David J. Schwartz
Publisher: Simon and Schuster Trade, January 1979
ISBN: 0671646788

The Richest Man in Babylon
Author: George S. Clason
Publisher: Dutton, February 1988
ISBN: 0451165209

Creative Visualization
Author: Shakti Gawain
Publisher: New World Library, May 1995
ISBN: 1880032627

Dare to Win
Author: John Canfield with Mark Victor Hansen
Publisher: Berkley Publishing Group, January 1995,
ISBN: 0425150763

Og Mandino's Great Trilogy: The Greatest Salesman in the World/ the Greatest Secret in the World/the Greatest Miracle in the World
Author: Og Mandino
Publisher: Frederick Fell Publishers, January 2002
ISBN: 0883910349

You Were Born Rich
Author: Bob Proctor
Publisher: McCrary Publishing Inc.

Life is Tremendous
Author: Charlie Jones
Publisher: Tyndale House Publishers, June 1981
ISBN: 0842321845

Acres Of Diamonds
Author: Russell H. Conwell
Publisher: Berkley Publishing Group, May 1982
ISBN: 051509028X

H) Understanding Men & Women's Differences

His Needs, Her Needs: Building an Affair-Proof Marriage
Author: Willard F. Harley
Publisher: Revell, Fleming H. Company, April 2001,
ISBN: 0800717880

Men Are from Mars, Women Are from Venus: A Practical Guide for Improving Communication and Getting What You Want in Your Relationships

Author: John Gray, Ph.D.
Publisher: Harper Trade, March 1992
ISBN: 006016848X

The Five Love Languages: How to Express Heartfelt Commitment to Your Mate
Author: Gary Chapman
Publisher: Northfield Publishing, October 1992
ISBN: 1881273156

I) Weight Loss

Make the Connection: Ten Steps to a Better Body and a Better Life
Authors: Bob Green and Oprah Winfrey, Julie Johnson (Illustrator)
Publisher: Hyperion, April 1999
ISBN: 0786882980

A Journal of Daily Renewal: The Companion to Make the Connection
Authors: Bob Greene & Oprah Winfrey
Publisher: Hyperion, September 1996
ISBN: 0786882158

Dr. Shapiro's Picture Perfect Weight Loss: The Visual Program for Permanent Weight Loss
Author: Howard M. Shapiro
Publisher: Rodale press, April 2000
ISBN: 1579542417

Fattitudes: Beat Self-Defeat and Win Your War with Weight
Authors: Jeffrey R. Wilbert & Norean K. Wilbert
Publisher: St. Martin's Press, Inc., May 2001
ISBN: 0312978812

Thin For Life: 10 Keys to Success from People Who Have Lost Weight and Kept It Off

Author: Anne M. Fletcher Foreword by Jane Brody
Publisher: Chapters Books, December 1994
ISBN: 1881527603

Reinventing Yourself with the Duchess of York: Inspiring Stories and Strategies for Changing Your Weight and Your Life
Author: Sarah the Duchess of York, Weight Watchers (Editor)
Publisher: Simon & Schuster Trade, December 2000,
ISBN: 0743213300

The 9 Truths about Weight Loss: The No-Tricks, No-Nonsense Plan for Lifelong Weight Control
Author: Daniel S. Kirschenbaum, Ph.D.
Publisher: Henry Holt & Company, Inc., March 2001,
ISBN: 0805063943

Appendix 2

Bible references

(All Bible quotes are taken from the New International Version)

A) Love your neighbor as yourself:

Leviticus 19:18

"Do not seek revenge or bear a grudge against one of your people, but love your neighbor as yourself. I am the LORD."

Matthew 22:37-40

Jesus replied: "'Love the Lord your God with all your heart and with all your soul and with all your mind.' This is the first and greatest commandment. And the second is like it: 'Love your neighbor as yourself.' All the Law and the Prophets hang on these two commandments."

Mark 12:29-31

"The most important one," answered Jesus, "is this: 'Hear, O Israel, the Lord our God, the Lord is one. Love the Lord your God with all your heart and with all your soul and with all your mind and with all your strength.' The second is this: 'Love your neighbor as yourself.' There is no commandment greater than these."

Luke 10:27-28

He answered: "'Love the Lord your God with all your heart and with all your soul and with all your strength and with all your mind'; and, 'Love your neighbor as yourself.'"

"You have answered correctly," Jesus replied. "Do this and you will live."

Romans 13:8-10

Let no debt remain outstanding, except the continuing debt to love one another, for he who loves his fellowman has fulfilled the law.

The commandments, "Do not commit adultery," "Do not murder," "Do not steal," "Do not covet," and whatever other commandment there may be, are summed up in this one rule: "Love your neighbor as yourself."

Love does no harm to its neighbor. Therefore love is the fulfillment of the law.

Galatians 5:14

The entire law is summed up in a single command: "Love your neighbor as yourself."

James 2:8

If you really keep the royal law found in Scripture, "Love your neighbor as yourself," you are doing right.

B) Cultivate a positive mental attitude:

Romans 12:2

Do not conform any longer to the pattern of this world, but be transformed by the renewing of your mind. Then you will be able to test and approve what God's will is—his good, pleasing and perfect will.

Philippians 4:8

Finally, brothers, whatever is true, whatever is noble, whatever is right, whatever is pure, whatever is lovely, whatever is admirable—if anything is excellent or praiseworthy—think about such things.

Luke 6:45

The good man brings good things out of the good stored up in his heart, and the evil man brings evil things out of the evil stored up in his heart. For out of the overflow of his heart his mouth speaks.

C) The Golden Rule:

Matthew 7:12

"So in everything, do to others what you would have them do to you, for this sums up the Law and the Prophets."

Luke 6:30-32

"Give to everyone who asks you, and if anyone takes what belongs to you, do not demand it back. Do to others as you would have them do to you. If you love those who love you, what credit is that to you? Even 'sinners' love those who love them."

D) How to treat others:

Luke 6:37-38

"Do not judge, and you will not be judged. Do not condemn, and you will not be condemned. Forgive, and you will be forgiven. Give, and it will be given to you. A good measure, pressed down, shaken together and running over, will be poured into your lap. For with the measure you use, it will be measured to you."

Romans 12:13-20

"Share with God's people who are in need. Practice hospitality. Bless those who persecute you; bless and do not curse. Rejoice with those who rejoice; mourn with those who mourn. Live in harmony with one another. Do not be proud, but be willing to associate with people of low position. Do not be conceited. Do not repay anyone evil for evil. Be careful to do what is right in the eyes of everybody. If it is possible, as far as it depends on you, live at peace with everyone. Do not take revenge, my friends, but leave room for God's wrath, for it is written: 'It is mine to avenge; I will repay,' says the Lord. On the contrary: 'If your enemy is hungry, feed him; if he is thirsty, give him something to drink. In doing this, you will heap burning coals on his head.'"

1 Peter 4:8-11

"Above all, love each other deeply, because love covers over a multitude of sins. Offer hospitality to one another without grumbling. Each one should use whatever gift he has received to serve others, faithfully administering God's grace in its various forms. If anyone speaks, he should do it as one speaking the very words of God. If anyone serves, he should do it with the strength God provides, so that in all things

God may be praised through Jesus Christ. To him be the glory and the power for ever and ever. Amen."

1 John 3:15-18

"Anyone who hates his brother is a murderer, and you know that no murderer has eternal life in him. This is how we know what love is: Jesus Christ laid down his life for us. And we ought to lay down our lives for our brothers. If anyone has material possessions and sees his brother in need but has no pity on him, how can the love of God be in him? Dear children, let us not love with words or tongue but with actions and in truth."

1 John 4:7-12

"Dear friends, let us love one another, for love comes from God. Everyone who loves has been born of God and knows God. Whoever does not love does not know God, because God is love. This is how God showed his love among us: He sent his one and only Son into the world that we might live through him. This is love: not that we loved God, but that he loved us and sent his Son as an atoning sacrifice for our sins. Dear friends, since God so loved us, we also ought to love one another. No one has ever seen God; but if we love one another, God lives in us and his love is made complete in us."

E) Genuine Believers:

Matt. 7:21-27

"Not everyone who says to me, 'Lord, Lord,' will enter the kingdom of heaven, but only he who does the will of my Father who is in heaven. Many will say to me on that day, 'Lord, Lord, did we not prophesy in your name, and in your name drive out demons and perform many miracles?' Then I will tell them plainly, 'I never knew you. Away from me, you evildoers!'"

Therefore everyone who hears these words of mine and puts them into practice is like a wise man who built his house on the rock. The rain came down, the streams rose, and the winds blew and beat against that house; yet it did not fall, because it had its foundation on the rock. But everyone who hears these words of mine and does not put them into practice is like a foolish man who built his house on sand. The rain came down, the streams rose, and the winds blew and beat against that house, and it fell with a great crash."

F) Control your tongue:

Job 15:4-6

"But you even undermine piety and hinder devotion to God. Your sin prompts your mouth; you adopt the tongue of the crafty. Your own mouth condemns you, not mine; your own lips testify against you."

Psalm 12:2-4

"Everyone lies to his neighbor; their flattering lips speak with deception. May the LORD cut off all flattering lips and every boastful tongue that says, 'We will triumph with our tongues; we own our lips—who is our master?'"

Psalm 15:1-5 (A psalm of David)

"LORD, who may dwell in your sanctuary? Who may live on your holy hill? He whose walk is blameless and who does what is righteous, who speaks the truth from his heart and has no slander on his tongue, who does his neighbor no wrong and casts no slur on his fellowman, who despises a vile man but honors those who fear the LORD, who keeps his oath even when it hurts, who lends his money without usury and does not accept a bribe against the innocent. He who does these things will never be shaken."

Psalm 34:12-14

"Whoever of you loves life and desires to see many good days, keep your tongue from evil and your lips from speaking lies. Turn from evil and do good; seek peace and pursue it."

Psalm 39:1

"I said, 'I will watch my ways and keep my tongue from sin; I will put a muzzle on my mouth as long as the wicked are in my presence.'"

Proverbs 6:16-18

"There are six things the LORD hates, seven that are detestable to him: haughty eyes, a lying tongue, hands that shed innocent blood, a heart that devises wicked schemes, feet that are quick to rush into evil."

Proverbs 10:18-20

"He who conceals his hatred has lying lips, and whoever spreads slander is a fool. When words are many, sin is not absent, but he who holds his tongue is wise. The tongue of the righteous is choice silver, but the heart of the wicked is of little value."

Proverbs 10:31-32

"The mouth of the righteous brings forth wisdom, but a perverse tongue will be cut out. The lips of the righteous know what is fitting, but the mouth of the wicked only what is perverse."

Proverbs 11:11-13

"Through the blessing of the upright a city is exalted, but by the mouth of the wicked it is destroyed.
A man who lacks judgment derides his neighbor, but a man of understanding holds his tongue. A gossip betrays a confidence, but a trustworthy man keeps a secret."

Proverbs 12:17-19

"A truthful witness gives honest testimony, but a false witness tells lies. Reckless words pierce like a sword, but the tongue of the wise brings healing. Truthful lips endure forever, but a lying tongue lasts only a moment."

Proverbs 15:1-2

"A gentle answer turns away wrath, but a harsh word stirs up anger. The tongue of the wise commends knowledge, but the mouth of the fool gushes folly."

Proverbs 15:4

"The tongue that brings healing is a tree of life, but a deceitful tongue crushes the spirit."

Proverbs 17:20

"A man of perverse heart does not prosper; he whose tongue is deceitful falls into trouble."

Proverbs 18:20-21

"From the fruit of his mouth a man's stomach is filled; with the harvest from his lips he is satisfied.
The tongue has the power of life and death, and those who love it will eat its fruit."

Proverbs 21:23

"He who guards his mouth and his tongue keeps himself from calamity."

James 1:26

"If anyone considers himself religious and yet does not keep a tight rein on his tongue, he deceives himself and his religion is worthless."

James 3:3-13

"When we put bits into the mouths of horses to make them obey us, we can turn the whole animal. Or take ships as an example. Although they are so large and are driven by strong winds, they are steered by a very small rudder wherever the pilot wants to go.

Likewise the tongue is a small part of the body, but it makes great boasts. Consider what a great forest is set on fire by a small spark. The tongue also is a fire, a world of evil among the parts of the body. It corrupts the whole person, sets the whole course of his life on fire, and is itself set on fire by hell.

All kinds of animals, birds, reptiles and creatures of the sea are being tamed and have been tamed by man, but no man can tame the tongue. It is a restless evil, full of deadly poison. With the tongue we praise our Lord and Father, and with it we curse men, who have been made in God's likeness. Out of the same mouth come praise and cursing. My brothers, this should not be. Can both fresh water and salt water flow from the same spring? My brothers, can a fig tree bear olives, or a grapevine bear figs? Neither can a salt spring produce fresh water.
Who is wise and understanding among you? Let him show it

by his good life, by deeds done in the humility that comes from wisdom."

G) Accept personal responsibility:

Galatians 6:3-5

"If anyone thinks he is something when he is nothing, he deceives himself. Each one should test his own actions. Then he can take pride in himself, without comparing himself to somebody else, for each one should carry his own load."

H) Do not be anxious:

Matt. 6:25-34

"Therefore I tell you, do not worry about your life, what you will eat or drink; or about your body, what you will wear. Is not life more important than food, and the body more important than clothes?

Look at the birds of the air; they do not sow or reap or store away in barns, and yet your heavenly Father feeds them. Are you not much more valuable than they? Who of you by worrying can add a single hour to his life?

And why do you worry about clothes? See how the lilies of the field grow. They do not labor or spin. Yet I tell you that not even Solomon in all his splendor was dressed like one of these. If that is how God clothes the grass of the field, which is here today and tomorrow is thrown into the fire, will he not much more clothe you, O you of little faith?

So do not worry, saying, 'What shall we eat?' or 'What shall we drink?' or 'What shall we wear?' For the pagans run after all these things, and your heavenly Father knows that you need them. But seek first his kingdom and his righteousness, and all these things will be given to you as well.

Therefore do not worry about tomorrow, for tomorrow will worry about itself. Each day has enough trouble of its own."

John 14:1 (Jesus speaking)

"Do not let your hearts be troubled. Trust in God; trust also in me."

Philippians 4:6-7

"Do not be anxious about anything, but in everything, by prayer and petition, with thanksgiving, present your requests to God. And the peace of God, which transcends all understanding, will guard your hearts and your minds in Christ Jesus."

I) Christians Married to Unbelievers:

1 Peter 3:1-2

"Wives, in the same way be submissive to your husbands so that, if any of them do not believe the word, they may be won over without words by the behavior of their wives, when they see the purity and reverence of your lives."

1 Corinthians 7:12-16

"To the rest I say this (I, not the Lord): If any brother has a wife who is not a believer and she is willing to live with him, he must not divorce her. And if a woman has a husband who is not a believer and he is willing to live with her, she must not divorce him. For the unbelieving husband has been sanctified through his wife, and the unbelieving wife has been sanctified through her believing husband. Otherwise your children would be unclean, but as it is, they are holy. But if the unbeliever leaves, let him do so. A believing man or woman is not bound in such circumstances; God has called us to live in peace. How do you know, wife, whether you will save your husband? Or, how do you know, husband, whether you will save your wife?"

J) Family relationships:

Colossians 3:18-21

"Wives, submit to your husbands, as is fitting in the Lord. Husbands, love your wives and do not be harsh with them. Children, obey your parents in everything, for this pleases the Lord. Fathers, do not embitter your children, or they will become discouraged."

1 Peter 3:1-7

"Wives, in the same way be submissive to your husbands . . . Your beauty should not come from outward adornment, such as braided hair and the wearing of gold jewelry and fine clothes. Instead, it should be that of your inner self, the unfading beauty of a gentle and quiet spirit, which is of great worth in God's sight. For this is the way the holy women of the past who put their hope in God used to make themselves beautiful. They were submissive to their own husbands, like Sarah, who obeyed Abraham and called him her master. You are her daughters if you do what is right and do not give way to fear.

Husbands, in the same way be considerate as you live with your wives, and treat them with respect as the weaker partner and as heirs with you of the gracious gift of life, so that nothing will hinder your prayers."

Titus 2:3-8

"Likewise, teach the older women to be reverent in the way they live, not to be slanderers or addicted to much wine, but to teach what is good. Then they can train the younger women to love their husbands and children, to be self-controlled and pure, to be busy at home, to be kind, and to be subject to their husbands, so that no one will malign the word of God.

Similarly, encourage the young men to be self-controlled. In everything set them an example by doing what is good. In your teaching show integrity, seriousness and soundness of speech that cannot be condemned, so that those who oppose you may be ashamed because they have nothing bad to say about us."

Ephesians 5:21-22, 24-25, 28-29, 33 & 6:1-4

"Submit to one another out of reverence for Christ. Wives, submit to your husbands as to the Lord . . . wives should submit to their husbands in everything.

Husbands, love your wives, just as Christ loved the church and gave himself up for her . . . husbands ought to love their wives as their own bodies. He who loves his wife loves himself. After all, no one ever hated his own body, but he feeds and cares for it . . . each one of you also must love his wife as he loves himself, and the wife must respect her husband.

Children, obey your parents in the Lord, for this is right. 'Honor your father and mother'—which is the first commandment with a promise—'that it may go well with you and that you may enjoy long life on the earth.'

Fathers, do not exasperate your children; instead, bring them up in the training and instruction of the Lord.''

1 Timothy 5:4 & 8

"But if a widow has children or grandchildren, these should learn first of all to put their religion into practice by caring for their own family and so repaying their parents and grandparents, for this is pleasing to God.

If anyone does not provide for his relatives, and especially for his immediate family, he has denied the faith and is worse than an unbeliever."

1 Timothy 5:14

"So I counsel younger widows to marry, to have children, to manage their homes and to give the enemy no opportunity for slander."

K) Do good for each other:

Galatians 6:9-10

"Let us not become weary in doing good, for at the proper time we will reap a harvest if we do not give up.
Therefore, as we have opportunity, let us do good to all people, especially to those who belong to the family of believers."

Ephesians 2:10

"For we are God's workmanship, created in Christ Jesus to do good works, which God prepared in advance for us to do."

1 Timothy 6:17-19

"Command those who are rich in this present world not to be arrogant nor to put their hope in wealth, which is so

uncertain, but to put their hope in God, who richly provides us with everything for our enjoyment.
Command them to do good, to be rich in good deeds, and to be generous and willing to share. In this way they will lay up treasure for themselves as a firm foundation for the coming age, so that they may take hold of the life that is truly life."

Hebrews 10:24

"And let us consider how we may spur one another on toward love and good deeds."

Galatians 6:2

"Carry each other's burdens, and in this way you will fulfill the law of Christ."

L) Sex in marriage:

1 Corinthians 7:3-5

"The husband should fulfill his marital duty to his wife, and likewise the wife to her husband. The wife's body does not belong to her alone but also to her husband. In the same way, the husband's body does not belong to him alone but also to his wife. Do not deprive each other except by mutual consent and for a time, so that you may devote yourselves to prayer. Then come together again so that Satan will not tempt you because of your lack of self-control."

Appendix 3

Supporting Documentation

A) Microwave Ovens (are they safe?)

Radiation Ovens—The Proven Dangers Of Microwaves
By Anthony Wayne and Lawrence Newell

    Is it possible that millions of people are ignorantly sacrificing their health in exchange for the convenience of microwave ovens? Why did the Soviet Union ban the use of microwave ovens in 1976? Who invented microwave ovens, and why? The answers to these questions may shock you into throwing your microwave oven in the trash.

    Over 90% of American homes have microwave ovens used for meal preparation. Because microwave ovens are so convenient and energy efficient, as compared to conventional ovens, very few homes or restaurants are without them. In general, people believe that whatever a microwave oven does to foods cooked in it doesn't have any negative effect on either the food or them. Of course, if microwave ovens were really harmful, our government would never allow them on the market, would they? Would they? Regardless of what has been "officially" released concerning microwave ovens, we have personally stopped using ours based on the research facts outlined in this article.

The purpose of this report is to show proof—evidence—that microwave cooking is not natural, nor healthy, and is far more dangerous to the human body than anyone could imagine. However, the microwave oven manufacturers, Washington City politics, and plain old human nature, are suppressing the facts and evidence. Because of this, people are continuing to microwave their food—in blissful ignorance—without knowing the effects and danger of doing so.

HOW DO MICROWAVE OVENS WORK?

Microwaves are a form of electromagnetic energy, like light waves or radio waves, and occupy a part of the electromagnetic spectrum of power, or energy. Microwaves are very short waves of electromagnetic energy that travel at the speed of light (186,282 miles per second). In our modern technological age, microwaves are used to relay long distance telephone signals, television programs, and computer information across the earth or to a satellite in space. But the microwave is most familiar to us as an energy source for cooking food.

Every microwave oven contains a magnetron, a tube in which electrons are affected by magnetic and electric fields in such a way as to produce micro wavelength radiation at about 2450 Mega Hertz (MHz) or 2.45 Giga Hertz (GHz). This microwave radiation interacts with the molecules in food. All wave energy changes polarity from positive to negative with each cycle of the wave. In microwaves, these polarity changes happen millions of times every second. Food molecules—especially the molecules of water—have a positive and negative end in the same way a magnet has a north and a south polarity.

In commercial models, the oven has a power input of about 1000 watts of alternating current. As these microwaves generated from the magnetron bombard the food, they cause the polar molecules to rotate at the same frequency millions of times a second. All this agitation creates molecular friction, which heats up the food. The friction also causes substantial damage to the surrounding molecules, often tearing them apart or forcefully deforming them. The scientific name for this deformation is "structural isomerism."

By comparison, microwaves from the sun are based on principles of pulsed direct current (DC) that don't create frictional heat; microwave ovens use alternating current (AC) creating frictional heat. A microwave oven produces a spiked wavelength of energy with all the power going into only one narrow frequency of the energy spectrum. Energy from the sun operates in a wide frequency spectrum.

Many terms are used in describing electromagnetic waves, such as wavelength, amplitude, cycle and frequency:

> WAVELENGTH determines the type of radiation, i.e. radio, X-ray, ultraviolet, visible, infrared, etc.
> AMPLITUDE determines the extent of movement measured from the starting point.
> CYCLE determines the unit of frequency, such as cycles per second, Hertz, Hz, or cycles/second.
> FREQUENCY determines the number of occurrences within a given time period (usually 1 second); The number of occurrences of a recurring process per unit of time, i.e. the number of repetitions of cycles per second.

RADIATION = SPREADING ENERGY WITH ELECTROMAGNETIC WAVES

Radiation, as defined by physics terminology, is "the electromagnetic waves emitted by the atoms and molecules of a radioactive substance as a result of nuclear decay." Radiation causes ionization, which is what occurs when a neutral atom gains or loses electrons. In simpler terms, a microwave oven decays and changes the molecular structure of the food by the process of radiation. Had the manufacturers accurately called them "radiation ovens," it's doubtful they would have ever sold one, but that's exactly what a microwave oven is.

We've all been told that microwaving food is not the same as irradiating it (radiation "treatment"). The two processes are supposed to use completely different waves of energy and at different intensities. No FDA or officially released government studies have proven current microwaving usage to be harmful, but we all know that the validity of studies can be—and are sometimes deliberately—limiting. Many of these studies are later proven to be inaccurate. As consumers, we're supposed to have a certain degree of common sense to use in judgment.

Take the example of eggs and how they were "proven" to be so harmful to our health in the late 1960's. This brought about imitation egg products and big profits for the manufacturers, while egg farms went broke. Now, recent government sponsored studies are saying that eggs are not bad for us after all. So, whom should we believe and what criteria should we use to decide matters concerning our health? Since it's currently published that microwaves—purportedly—don't leak into the environment, when properly used and with approved design, the decision lies with each consumer as to whether or not you choose to eat food heated by a microwave oven or even purchase one in the first place.

MOTHERLY INSTINCTS ARE RIGHT

On a more humorous side, the "sixth sense" every mother has is impossible to argue with. Have you ever tried it? Children will never win against a mother's intuition. It's like trying to argue with the arm—appearing out of nowhere—

that pinned you to the back of the seat when your mother slammed on the brakes.

Many of us come from a generation where mothers and grandmothers have distrusted the modern "inside out" cooking they claimed was "not suitable" for most foods. My mother refused to even try baking anything in a microwave. She also didn't like the way a cup of coffee tasted when heated in a microwave oven. I have to fully agree and can't argue either fact. Her own common sense and instincts told her that there was no way microwave cooking could be natural nor make foods "taste they way they're supposed to." Reluctantly, even my mother succumbed to re-heating leftovers in a microwave due to her work schedule before she retired.

Many others feel the same way, but they're considered an "old fashioned" minority dating back to before the 1970's when microwaves first overwhelmed the market. Like most young adults at the time, as microwave ovens became commonplace, I chose to ignore my mother's intuitive wisdom and joined the majority who believed microwave cooking was far too convenient to ever believe anything could be wrong with it. Chalk one up for mom's perception, because even though she didn't know the scientific, technical, or health reasons why, she just knew that microwave ovens were not good based on how foods tasted when they were cooked in them. She didn't like the way the texture of the microwaved food changed either.

MICROWAVES UNSAFE FOR BABY'S MILK

A number of warnings have been made public, but have been barely noticed. For example, Young Families, the Minnesota Extension Service of the University of Minnesota, published the following in 1989:

"Although microwaves heat food quickly, they are not recommended for heating a baby's bottle. The bottle may seem cool to the touch, but the liquid inside may become extremely hot and could burn the baby's mouth and throat. Also, the buildup of steam in a closed container, such as a baby bottle, could cause it to explode. Heating the bottle in a microwave can cause slight changes in the milk. In infant formulas, there may be a loss of some vitamins. In expressed breast milk, some protective properties may be destroyed. Warming a bottle by holding it under tap water, or by setting it in a bowl of warm water, then testing it on your wrist before feeding may take a few minutes longer, but it is much safer."

Dr. Lita Lee of Hawaii reported in the December 9, 1989 Lancet:

"Microwaving baby formulas converted certain trans-amino acids into their synthetic cis-isomers. Synthetic isomers, whether cis-amino acids or trans-fatty acids, are not biologically active. Further, one of the amino acids, L-proline, was converted to its d-isomer, which is known to be neurotoxic (poisonous to the nervous system) and nephrotoxic (poisonous to the kidneys). It's bad enough that many babies are not nursed, but now they are given fake milk (baby formula) made even more toxic via microwaving."

MICROWAVED BLOOD KILLS PATIENT

In 1991, there was a lawsuit in Oklahoma concerning the hospital use of a microwave oven to warm blood needed in a transfusion. The case involved a hip surgery patient, Norma Levitt, who died from a simple blood transfusion. It seems the nurse had warmed the blood in a microwave oven. This tragedy makes it very apparent that there's much more to "heating" with microwaves than we've been led to believe. Blood for transfusions is routinely warmed, but not in microwave ovens. In the case of Mrs. Levitt, the microwaving altered the blood and it killed her.

It's very obvious that this form of microwave radiation "heating" does something to the substances it heats. It's also becoming quite apparent that people who process food in a microwave oven are also ingesting these "unknowns."

Because the body is electrochemical in nature, any force that disrupts or changes human electrochemical events will affect the physiology of the body. This is further described in Robert O. Becker's book, The Body Electric, and in Ellen Sugarman's book, Warning, the Electricity Around You May Be Hazardous to Your Health.

SCIENTIFIC EVIDENCE AND FACTS

In Comparative Study of Food Prepared Conventionally and in the Microwave Oven, published by Raum & Zelt in 1992, at 3(2): 43, it states:

"A basic hypothesis of natural medicine states that the introduction into the human body of molecules and energies, to which it is not accustomed, is much more likely to cause harm than good. Microwaved food contains both molecules and energies not present in food cooked in the way humans have been cooking food since the discovery of fire. Microwave energy from the sun and other stars is direct current based. Artificially produced microwaves, including those in ovens, are produced from alternating current and force a billion or more polarity reversals per second in every food molecule they hit. Production of unnatural molecules is inevitable. Naturally occurring amino acids have been observed to undergo isomeric changes (changes in shape morphing) as well as transformation into toxic forms, under the impact of microwaves produced in ovens.

One short-term study found significant and disturbing changes in the blood of individuals consuming microwaved milk and vegetables. Eight volunteers ate various combinations of the same foods cooked different ways. All foods that were processed through the microwave ovens caused changes in the blood of the volunteers. Hemoglobin levels decreased and over all white cell levels and cholesterol levels increased. Lymphocytes decreased.

Luminescent (light-emitting) bacteria were employed to detect energetic changes in the blood. Significant increases were found in the luminescence of these bacteria when exposed to blood serum obtained after the consumption of microwaved food."

THE SWISS CLINICAL STUDY

Dr. Hans Ulrich Hertel, who is now retired, worked as a food scientist for many years with one of the major Swiss food companies that do business on a global scale. A few years ago, he was fired from his job for questioning certain processing procedures that denatured the food.

In 1991, he and a Lausanne University professor published a research paper indicating that food cooked in microwave ovens could pose a greater risk to health than food cooked by conventional means. An article also appeared in issue 19 of the Journal Franz Weber in which it was stated that the consumption of food cooked in microwave ovens had cancerous effects on the blood. The research paper itself followed the article. On the cover of the magazine there was a picture of the Grim Reaper holding a microwave oven in one of his hands.

Dr. Hertel was the first scientist to conceive and carry out a quality clinical study on the effects microwaved nutrients have on the blood and physiology of the human body. His small but well controlled study showed the degenerative force produced in microwave ovens and the food processed in them. The scientific conclusion showed that microwave cooking changed the nutrients in the food; and, changes took place in the participants' blood that could cause deterioration in the human system. Hertel's scientific study was done along with Dr. Bernard H. Blanc of the Swiss Federal

Institute of Technology and the University Institute for Biochemistry.

In intervals of two to five days, the volunteers in the study received one of the following food variants on an empty stomach: (1) raw milk; (2) the same milk conventionally cooked; (3) pasteurized milk; (4) the same raw milks cooked in a microwave oven; (5) raw vegetables from an organic farm; (6) the same vegetables cooked conventionally; (7) the same vegetables frozen and defrosted in a microwave oven; and (8) the same vegetables cooked in the microwave oven. Once the volunteers were isolated, blood samples were taken from every volunteer immediately before eating. Then, blood samples were taken at defined intervals after eating from the above milk or vegetable preparations.

Significant changes were discovered in the blood samples from the intervals following the foods cooked in the microwave oven. These changes included a decrease in all hemoglobin and cholesterol values, especially the ratio of HDL (good cholesterol) and LDL (bad cholesterol) values. Lymphocytes (white blood cells) showed a more distinct short-term decrease following the intake of microwaved food than after the intake of all the other variants. Each of these indicators pointed to degeneration. Additionally, there was a highly significant association between the amount of microwave energy in the test foods and the luminous power of luminescent bacteria exposed to serum from test persons who ate that food. This led Dr. Hertel to the conclusion that such technically derived energies may, indeed, be passed along to man inductively via eating microwaved food.

According to Dr. Hertel,

"Leukocytosis, which cannot be accounted for by normal daily deviations, is taken very seriously by hematologists.

Leukocytes are often signs of pathogenic effects on the living system, such as poisoning and cell damage. The increase of leukocytes with the microwaved foods were more pronounced than with all the other variants. It appears that these marked increases were caused entirely by ingesting the microwaved substances.

This process is based on physical principles and has already been confirmed in the literature. The apparent additional energy exhibited by the luminescent bacteria was merely an extra confirmation. There is extensive scientific literature concerning the hazardous effects of direct microwave radiation on living systems. It is astonishing, therefore, to realize how little effort has been taken to replace this detrimental technique of microwaves with technology more in accordance with nature. Technically produced microwaves are based on the principle of alternating current. Atoms, molecules, and cells hit by this hard electromagnetic radiation are forced to reverse polarity 1-100 billion times a second. There are no atoms, molecules or cells of any organic system able to withstand such a violent, destructive power for any extended period of time, not even in the low energy range of milliwatts.

Of all the natural substances—which are polar—the oxygen of water molecules reacts most sensitively. This is how microwave cooking heat is generated—friction from this violence in water molecules. Structures of molecules are torn apart, molecules are forcefully deformed, called structural isomerism, and thus become impaired in quality. This is contrary to conventional heating of food where heat transfers convectionally from without to within. Cooking by microwaves begins within the cells and molecules where water is present and where the energy is transformed into frictional heat.

In addition to the violent frictional heat effects, called thermic effects, there are also athermic effects which have hardly ever been taken into account. These athermic effects are not presently measurable, but they can also deform the structures of molecules and have qualitative consequences. For example the weakening of cell membranes by microwaves is used in the field of gene altering technology. Because of the force involved, the cells are actually broken, thereby neutralizing the electrical potentials, the very life of the cells, between the outer and inner side of the cell membranes. Impaired cells become easy prey for viruses, fungi and other microorganisms. The natural repair mechanisms are suppressed and cells are forced to adapt to a state of energy emergency—they switch from aerobic to anaerobic respiration. Instead of water and carbon dioxide, the cell poisons hydrogen peroxide and carbon monoxide are produced."

The same violent deformations that occur in our bodies, when we are directly exposed to radar or microwaves, also occur in the molecules of foods cooked in a microwave oven. This radiation results in the destruction and deformation of food molecules. Microwaving also creates new compounds, called radiolytic compounds, which are unknown fusions not found in nature. Radiolytic compounds are created by molecular decomposition—decay—as a direct result of radiation.

Microwave oven manufacturers insist that microwaved and irradiated foods do not have any significantly higher radiolytic compounds than do broiled, baked or other conventionally cooked foods. The scientific clinical evidence presented here has shown that this is simply a lie. In America, neither universities nor the federal government have conducted any tests concerning the effects on our bodies from eating microwaved foods. Isn't that a bit odd? They're more concerned with studies on what happens if the door on a microwave oven doesn't close properly. Once again, common sense tells us that their attention should be centered on what happens to food cooked inside a microwave oven. Since people ingest this altered food, shouldn't there be concern for how the same decayed molecules will affect our own human biological cell structure?

INDUSTRY'S ACTION TO HIDE THE TRUTH

As soon as Doctors Hertel and Blanc published their results, the authorities reacted. A powerful trade organization, the Swiss Association of Dealers for Electro-apparatuses for Households and Industry, known as FEA, struck swiftly in 1992. They forced the President of the Court of Seftigen, Canton of Bern, to issue a "gag order" against Drs. Hertel and Blanc. In March 1993, Dr. Hertel was convicted for "interfering with commerce" and prohibited from further publishing his results. However, Dr. Hertel stood his ground and fought this decision over the years.

Not long ago, this decision was reversed in a judgment delivered in Strasbourg, Austria, on August 25, 1998. The European Court of Human Rights held that there had been a violation of Hertel's rights in the 1993 decision. The European Court of Human Rights also ruled that the "gag order" issued by the Swiss court in 1992 against Dr. Hertel, prohibiting him from declaring that microwave ovens are dangerous to human health, was contrary to the right to freedom of expression. In addition, Switzerland was ordered to pay Dr. Hertel compensation.

WHO INVENTED MICROWAVE OVENS?

The Nazis, for use in their mobile support operations, originally developed microwave "radiomissor" cooking ovens to be used for the invasion of Russia. By being able to utilize electronic equipment for preparation of meals on a mass scale, the logistical problem of cooking fuels would have been eliminated, as well as the convenience of producing edible products in a greatly reduced time-factor.

After the war, the Allies discovered medical research done by the Germans on microwave ovens. These documents, along with some working microwave ovens, were transferred to the United States War Department and classified for reference and "further scientific investigation." The Russians had also retrieved some microwave ovens and now have thorough research on their biological effects. As a result, their use was outlawed in the Soviet Union. The Soviets issued an international warning on the health hazards, both biological and environmental, of microwave ovens and similar frequency electronic devices.

Other Eastern European scientists also reported the harmful effects of microwave radiation and set up strict environmental limits for their usage. The United States has not accepted the European reports of harmful effects, even though the EPA estimates that radio frequency and microwave radiation sources in America are increasing at 15% per year.

CARCINOGENS IN MICROWAVED FOOD

In Dr. Lita Lee's book, Health Effects of Microwave Radiation—Microwave Ovens, and in the March and September 1991 issues of Earthletter, she stated that every microwave oven leaks electro-magnetic radiation, harms food, and converts substances cooked in it to dangerous organ-toxic and carcinogenic products. Further research summarized in this article reveal that microwave ovens are far more harmful than previously imagined.

The following is a summary of the Russian investigations published by the Atlantis Raising Educational Center in Portland, Oregon. Carcinogens were formed in virtually all foods tested. No test food was subjected to more microwaving than necessary to accomplish the purpose, i.e., cooking, thawing, or heating to insure sanitary ingestion. Here's a summary of some of the results:

- Microwaving prepared meats sufficiently to insure sanitary ingestion caused formation of d-Nitrosodienthanolamines, a well-known carcinogen.
- Microwaving milk and cereal grains converted some of their amino acids into carcinogens.
- Thawing frozen fruits converted their glucoside and galactoside containing fractions into carcinogenic substances.
- Extremely short exposure of raw, cooked or frozen vegetables converted their plant alkaloids into carcinogens.
- Carcinogenic free radicals were formed in microwaved plants, especially root vegetables.

DECREASE IN NUTRITIONAL VALUE

Russian researchers also reported a marked acceleration of structural degradation leading to a decreased food value of 60 to 90% in all foods tested. Among the changes observed were:

- Deceased bio-availability of vitamin B complex, vitamin C, vitamin E, essential minerals and lipotropics factors in all food tested.
- Various kinds of damaged [*sic*] to many plant substances, such as alkaloids, glucosides, galactosides and nitrilosides.
- The degradation of nucleo-proteins in meats.

MICROWAVE SICKNESS IS DISCOVERED

The Russians did research on thousands of workers who had been exposed to microwaves during the development of radar in the 1950's. Their research showed health problems so serious that the Russians set strict limits of 10 microwatts exposure for workers and one microwatt for civilians.

In Robert O. Becker's book, The Body Electric, he described Russian research on the health effects of microwave radiation, which they called "microwave sickness." On page 314, Becker states:

"It's [Microwave sickness] first signs are low blood pressure and slow pulse. The later and most common manifestations are chronic excitation of the sympathetic nervous system [stress syndrome] and high blood pressure. This phase also often includes headache, dizziness, eye pain, sleeplessness, irritability, anxiety, stomach pain, nervous tension, inability to concentrate, hair loss, plus an increased incidence of appendicitis, cataracts, reproductive problems, and cancer. The chronic symptoms are eventually succeeded by crisis of adrenal exhaustion and ischemic heart disease [the blockage of coronary arteries and heart attacks]."

According to Dr. Lee, changes are observed in the blood chemistries and the rates of certain diseases among consumers of microwaved foods. The symptoms above can easily be caused by the observations shown below. The following is a sample of these changes:

+ Lymphatic disorders were observed, leading to decreased ability to prevent certain types of cancers.
+ An increased rate of cancer cell formation was observed in the blood.
+ Increased rates of stomach and intestinal cancers were observed.
+ Higher rates of digestive disorders and a gradual breakdown of the systems of elimination were observed.

MICROWAVE RESEARCH CONCLUSIONS

The following were the most significant German and Russian research operations facilities concerning the biological effects of microwaves:

The initial research conducted by the Germans during the Barbarossa military campaign, at the Humbolt-Universitat zu Berlin (1942-1943); and,

From 1957 and up to the present [until the end of the cold war], the Russian research operations were conducted at: the Institute of Radio Technology at Kinsk, Byelorussian Autonomous Region; and, at the Institute of Radio Technology at Rajasthan in the Rossiskaja Autonomous Region, both in the Union of the Soviet Socialist Republics.

In most cases, the foods used for research analysis were exposed to microwave propagation at an energy potential of 100 kilowatts/cm3/second, to the point considered acceptable for sanitary, normal ingestion. The effects noted by both German and Russian researchers is presented in three categories:

CATEGORY I, Cancer-Causing Effects CATEGORY II, Nutritive Destruction of Foods CATEGORY III, Biological Effects of Exposure

CATEGORY I

CANCER-CAUSING EFFECTS

[The first two points of Category I are not readable from our report copy. The remainder of the report is intact.]

3. Creation of a "binding effect" to radioactivity in the atmosphere, thus causing a marked increase in the amount of alpha and beta particle saturation in foods;
4. Creation of cancer causing agents within protein hydrolysate compounds* in milk and cereal grains [*these are natural proteins that are split into unnatural fragments by the addition of water];
5. Alteration of elemental food substances, causing disorders in the digestive system by unstable catabolism* of foods subjected to microwaves [* the metabolic breakdown process];

6. Due to chemical alterations within food substances, malfunctions were observed within the lymphatic systems [absorbent vessels], causing a degeneration of the immune potentials of the body to protect against certain forms of neoplastics [abnormal growths of tissue];
7. Ingestion of microwaved foods caused a higher percentage of cancerous cells within the blood serum [cytomas—cell tumors such as sarcoma];
8. Microwave emissions caused alteration in the catabolic [metabolic breakdown] behavior of glucoside [hydrolyzed dextrose] and galactoside [oxidized alcohol] elements within frozen fruits when thawed in this manner;
9. Microwave emission caused alteration of the catabolic [metabolic breakdown] behavior of plant alkaloids [organic nitrogen based elements] when raw, cooked, or frozen vegetables were exposed for even extremely short durations;
10. Cancer causing free radicals [highly reactive incomplete molecules] were formed within certain trace mineral molecular formations in plant substances, and in particular, raw root-vegetables; and,
11. In a statistically high percentage of persons, microwaved foods caused stomach and intestinal cancerous growths, as well as a general degeneration of peripheral cellular tissues, with a gradual breakdown of the function of the digestive and excretive systems.

CATEGORY II

DECREASE IN FOOD VALUE

Microwave exposure caused significant decreases in the nutritive value of all foods researched. The following are the most important findings:

1. A decrease in the bioavailability [capability of the body to utilize the nutriment] of B-complex vitamins, Vitamin C, Vitamin E, essential minerals and lipotropics in all foods;
2. A loss of 60-90% of the vital energy field content of all tested foods;
3. A reduction in the metabolic behavior and integration process capability of alkaloids [organic nitrogen based elements], glucosides and galactosides, and nitrilosides;
4. A destruction of the nutritive value of nucleoproteins in meats;
5. A marked acceleration of structural disintegration in all foods.

CATEGORY III

BIOLOGICAL EFFECTS OF EXPOSURE

Exposure to microwave emissions also had an unpredictably negative effect upon the general biological welfare of humans. This was not discovered until the Russians experimented with highly sophisticated equipment and discovered that a human did not even need to ingest the material substance of the microwaved food substances: that even exposure to the energy field itself was sufficient to cause such adverse side effects that the use of any such microwave apparatus was forbidden in 1976 by Soviet state law.

The following are the enumerated effects:

1. A breakdown of the human "life-energy field" in those who were exposed to microwave ovens while in operation, with side-effects to the human energy field of increasingly longer duration;
2. A degeneration of the cellular voltage parallels during the process of using the apparatus, especially in the blood and lymphatic areas;

3. A degeneration and destabilization of the external energy activated potentials of food utilization within the processes of human metabolism;
4. A degeneration and destabilization of internal cellular membrane potentials while transferring catabolic [metabolic breakdown] processes into the blood serum from the digestive process;
5. Degeneration and circuit breakdowns of electrical nerve impulses within the junction potentials of the cerebrum [the front portion of the brain where thought and higher functions reside];
6. A degeneration and breakdown of nerve electrical circuits and loss of energy field symmetry in the neuroplexuses [nerve centers] both in the front and the rear of the central and autonomic nervous systems;
7. Loss of balance and circuiting of the bioelectric strengths within the ascending reticular activating system [the system which controls the function of consciousness];
8. A long term cumulative loss of vital energies within humans, animals and plants that were located within a 500-meter radius of the operational equipment;
9. Long lasting residual effects of magnetic "deposits" were located throughout the nervous system and lymphatic system;
10. A destabilization and interruption in the production of hormones and maintenance of hormonal balance in males and females;
11. Markedly higher levels of brainwave disturbance in the alpha, theta, and delta wave signal patterns of persons exposed to microwave emission fields, and;
12. Because of this brainwave disturbance, negative psychological effects were noted, including loss of memory, loss of ability to concentrate, suppressed emotional threshold, deceleration of intellective processes, and interruptive sleep episodes in a statistically higher percentage of individuals subjected to continual range

emissive field effects of microwave apparatus, either in cooking apparatus or in transmission stations.

FORENSIC RESEARCH CONCLUSIONS

From the twenty-eight above enumerated indications, the use of microwave apparatus is definitely not advisable; and, with the decision of the Soviet government in 1976, present scientific opinion in many countries concerning the use of such apparatus is clearly in evidence.

Due to the problem of random magnetic residulation and binding within the biological systems of the body (Category III:9), which can ultimately effect the neurological systems, primarily the brain and neuroplexuses (nerve centers), long term depolarization of tissue neuroelectric circuits can result. Because these effects can cause virtually irreversible damage to the neuroelectrical integrity of the various components of the nervous system (I. R. Luria, Novosibirsk 1975a), ingestion of microwaved foods is clearly contraindicated in all respects. Their magnetic residual effect can render the pyschoneural receptor components of the brain more subject to influence psychologically by artificially induced microwave radio frequency fields from transmission stations and TV relay-networks.

The theoretical possibility of psycho telemetric influence (the capability of affecting human behavior by transmitted radio signals at controlled frequencies) has been suggested by Soviet neuropsychological investigations at Uralyera and Novosibirsk (Luria and Perov, 1974a, 1975c, 1976a), which can cause involuntary subliminal psychological energy field compliance to operative microwave apparatus.
FORENSIC RESEARCH DOCUMENT Prepared By: William P. Kopp A. R. E. C. Research Operations TO61-7R10/10-77F05 RELEASE PRIORITY: CLASS I ROO1a

TEN REASONS TO THROW OUT YOUR MICROWAVE OVEN

From the conclusions of the Swiss, Russian and German scientific clinical studies, we can no longer ignore the microwave oven sitting in our kitchens. Based on this research, we will conclude this article with the following:

1). Continually eating food processed from a microwave oven causes long term—permanent—brain damage by "shorting out" electrical impulses in the brain [depolarizing or de-magnetizing the brain tissue].
2). The human body cannot metabolize [break down] the unknown by-products created in microwaved food.
3). Male and female hormone production is shut down and/or altered by continually eating microwaved foods.
4). The effects of microwaved food by-products are residual [long term, permanent] within the human body.
5). Minerals, vitamins, and nutrients of all microwaved food is reduced or altered so that the human body gets little or no benefit, or the human body absorbs altered compounds that cannot be broken down.
6). The minerals in vegetables are altered into cancerous free radicals when cooked in microwave ovens.
7). Microwaved foods cause stomach and intestinal cancerous growths [tumors]. This may explain the rapidly increased rate of colon cancer in America.
8). The prolonged eating of microwaved foods causes cancerous cells to increase in human blood.
9). Continual ingestion of microwaved food causes immune system deficiencies through lymph gland and blood serum alterations.
10). Eating microwaved food causes loss of memory, concentration, emotional instability, and a decrease of intelligence.

HAVE YOU TOSSED OUT YOUR MICROWAVE OVEN YET?

The use of artificial microwave transmissions for subliminal psychological control, a.k.a. "brainwashing," has also been proven. We're attempting to obtain copies of the 1970's Russian research documents and results written by Drs. Luria and Perov specifying their clinical experiments in this area.

> Written by Anthony Wayne and Lawrence Newell
> International common Law Copyright 2000 by the
> Christian Law Institute and Fellowship Assembly
> Reprinted with permission of the Christian Law
> Institute, *http://ecclesia.org* Contact: *info@lawgiver.org*

B) Dairy Products

There is some controversy surrounding the subject of dairy products and whether they are good for humans or not. To complicate things, the dairy industry (in America at least) has been involved in practices that increase milk production but which are questionable as to the long term health effects on humans. It is up to you to decide if you want to make dairy products a part of your diet or not. The following are some resources for you to check out to help you in that decision:

> *MILK: The Deadly Poison* by Robert Cohen
> ISBN # 0-9659-196-0-9
> Copyright © 1997 Argus Publishing
> 325 Sylvan Avenue
> Englewood Cliffs, NJ 07032
> Dairy Education Board
> 325 Sylvan Avenue
> Englewood Cliffs, NJ 07632

Phone: 201-871-5871
Fax: 201-871-9304
Email: *workshops@notmilk.com*
Website: *http://www.notmilk.com/*

C) TALC: Questions and Answers

Q. What is talc?

A. Talc is a mineral, produced by the mining of talc rocks and then processed by crushing, drying and milling. Processing eliminates a number of trace minerals from the talc, but does not separate minute fibers which are very similar to asbestos.

Q. What kinds of consumer products contain talc?

A. Talc is found in a wide variety of consumer products ranging from home and garden pesticides to antacids. However, the products most widely used and that pose the most serious health risks are body powders Talc is the main ingredient in baby powder, medicated powders, perfumed powders and designer perfumed body powders. Because talc is resistant to moisture, it is also used by the pharmaceutical industry to manufacture medications and is a listed ingredient of some antacids. Talc is the principal ingredient home and garden pesticides and flea and tick powders. Talc is used in smaller quantities in deodorants, chalk, crayons, textiles, soap, insulating materials, paints, asphalt filler, paper, and in food processing.

Q. Why is talc harmful?

A. Talc is closely related to the potent carcinogen asbestos. Talc particles have been shown to cause tumors in the ovaries and lungs of cancer victims. For the last 30 years, scientists have closely scrutinized talc particles and found dangerous similarities to asbestos. Responding to this evidence in 1973, the FDA drafted a resolution that would limit the amount of asbestos-like fibers in cosmetic grade talc. However, no ruling has ever been made and today, cosmetic grade talc remains non-regulated by the federal government. This inaction ignores a 1993 National Toxicology Program report which found that cosmetic grade talc, without any asbestos-like fibers, caused tumors in animal subjects. *Clearly with or without asbestos-like fibers, cosmetic grade talcum powder is a carcinogen.*

Q. What kind of exposure is dangerous?

A. Talc is toxic. Talc particles cause tumors in human ovaries and lungs. Numerous studies have shown a strong link between frequent use of talc in the female genital area and **ovarian cancer.** Talc particles are able to move through the reproductive system and become imbedded in the lining of the ovary. Researchers have found talc particles in ovarian tumors and have found that women with ovarian cancer have used talcum powder in their genital area more frequently than healthy women.

Talc poses a health risk when exposed to the lungs. Talc miners have shown higher rates of lung cancer and other respiratory illnesses from exposure to industrial grade talc, which contains dangerous silica and asbestos. The common household hazard posed by talc is inhalation of baby powder by infants. Since the early 1980s, records show that several thousand infants each year have died or become seriously ill following accidental inhalation of baby powder.

Q. What about infants?

A. Talc is used on babies because it absorbs unpleasant

moisture. Clearly, dusting with talcum powder endangers an infant's lungs at the prospect of inhalation. *Exposing children to this carcinogen is unnecessary and dangerous.*

HERE ARE THREE THINGS THAT YOU CAN DO:

1. **Do not buy or use products containing talc.** It is especially important that women not apply talc to underwear or sanitary pads.
2. **Contact your pediatrician and/or local hospital** and find out if they have a policy regarding talc use and infants.
3. **Write to the FDA and express your concern** that a proven carcinogen has remained unregulated while millions of people are unknowingly exposed.

FOR MORE INFORMATION:

Cancer Prevention Coalition c/o School of Public Health
University of Illinois Medical Center
2121 West Taylor Street
Chicago, IL 60612
Tel: (312) 996-2297, Fax: (312) 996-1374
Email: epstein@uic.edu

References:

1. National Toxicology Program. "Toxicology and carcinogenesis studies of talc (GAS N0 14807-96-6) in F344/N rats and B6C3F, mice (Inhalation studies)." *Technical Report Series N0 421.* September 1993.
2. Harlow BL, Cramer DW, Bell DA, Welch WR. "Perineal exposure to talc and ovarian cancer risk." *Obstetrics and Gynecology,* 80: 19-26, 1992.

3. Hollinger MA "Pulmonary toxicity of inhaled and intravenous talc" *Toxicology letters,* 52: 121~127, 1990.

D) Affirmations Based on Scripture

The Fruit of the Spirit

The Fruit of the Spirit is manifest in my life which is love, joy, peace, perseverance, kindness, goodness, faithfulness, gentleness, and self-control. (Galatians 5:22-23)
These are the qualities of love that are evident in my life; love is patient and kind. Having love in my life makes me secure; love makes me see myself in the proper perspective, love always acts appropriately; love remains calm in the face of adversity, love makes me easily let go of anger; love rejoices with righteousness and truth. Love preservers and believes the best in every situation. Love is full of hope, and is steadfast. Love never fails. (I Corinthians 13:4-8)
I love God with all of my heart, soul and mind. I love myself in the proper way; therefore I am able to love others. (Matthew 22:37-38)
I am full of joy and happiness all the time. I wake up joyful every morning and go to sleep happy every night. I rejoice in the Lord always. (Philippians 3:1)
I am anxious for nothing, because with thanksgiving, I always let my requests be made known to God through prayer. Therefore, the peace of God, which surpasses all comprehension, guards my heart and my mind in Christ Jesus. (Philippians 4:6-7)
Having been justified by faith, I have peace with God through my Lord Jesus Christ, through whom I also have obtained my introduction by faith into this grace in which I stand; and I exult in the hope of the glory of God. And not only this, but I also exult in my tribulations, knowing that tribulation brings about perseverance; and perseverance,

proven character; and proven character, hope, and hope does not disappoint, because the love of God has been poured out within my heart through the Holy Spirit who was given to me. (Romans 5:1-5)

I open my mouth in wisdom and the teaching of kindness in on my tongue. I extend a hand to the poor and I stretch out my hands to the needy. (Proverbs 31:26 and 20)

I apply all diligence and in my faith I supply moral excellence, and in moral excellence, knowledge; and in knowledge, self-control; and in self-control, perseverance, and in perseverance, godliness; and in godliness, brotherly kindness, and in brotherly kindness, Christian love. These qualities are mine and are increasing, and they render me fruitful in the true knowledge of my Lord Jesus Christ. (2 Peter 1:5-8)

The Lord will repay me for my faithfulness. I am faithful; therefore I will abound with blessings. (Psalm 37:28, Proverbs 28:20)

I am kind to others, and tenderhearted. I always forgive others, just as God in Christ has also forgiven me. (Ephesians 4:32)

I have the wisdom from above which is first pure, then peaceable, gentle, reasonable, full of mercy and good fruits, unwavering and genuine. (James 3:17)

Positive Attitude Affirmation

These are the things I think about; whatever is true, whatever is noble, whatever is right, whatever is pure, whatever is lovely, whatever is admirable and anything that is excellent or praiseworthy. (Philippians 4:8)

I banish anxiety from my heart and cast off the troubles of my body. I set my mind on heavenly things, not on earthly things. (Ecclesiastes 11:10, Colossians 3:2)

My heart is happy and my face is cheerful. (Proverbs 15:13)

I trust in God, therefore my mind is steady and at peace. (Isaiah 3:23)

I love the Lord my God with all my heart and with all my soul and with all my mind and with all my strength, and I love others as I love myself. (Mark 12:30)

My mind is controlled by the Spirit of God therefore I have life and peace. (Romans 8:6)

I am made new in Christ in the attitude of my mind and I have put on a new self that is created to be like God in true righteousness and holiness. (Ephesians 4:23-24)

I am continually growing in the grace and knowledge of my Lord and Savior Jesus Christ. (2 Peter 3:18)

Positive Behavior Affirmation

I do not conform any longer to the pattern of this world, but I am transformed by the renewing of my mind. (Romans 12:2)

I am sincere in my love. I hate what is evil and cling to what is good. I am enthusiastic but I don't overdo it. I am joyful in hope, patient in affliction and faithful in prayer. I share with God's people who are in need. I practice hospitality. I bless those who persecute me; I bless and do not curse. I rejoice with those who rejoice and mourn with those who mourn. I live in harmony with others. I am humble and don't ever think I am too good to associate with someone who has less money than I do. I do not repay anyone evil for evil. I am careful to do what is right. As much as it is possible, as far as it depends on me, I live at peace with everyone. I do not take revenge, but understand that God will take care of such things. I do not allow myself to be overcome with evil, but I overcome evil with good. (Romans 12:9-21)

I clothe myself with compassion, kindness, humility, gentleness and patience. I forgive others because I know that the Lord has forgiven me. (Colossians 3:12-13)

Whatever I do, I work at it with all my heart, as working for the Lord, not for men. (Colossians 3:23)

I have put off falsehood and I speak truthfully to others. When I am angry, I do not sin. I let go of my anger before I go to bed at night. I put my hands to useful work and I share with those in need. I guard my mouth and the words that I say are those that are helpful for building others up as they need it. What I say benefits those who listen. I have rid myself of all bitterness, rage and anger, brawling and slander, and also all forms of malice. I am kind and compassionate to others and I forgive others just as in Christ God forgave me. (Ephesians 4:25-32)

E) Studies on Attitude

1) "Optimism is Associated With Mood, Coping, and Immune Change in Response to Stress," *Journal of Personality and Social Psychology,* Volume 74, Number 6, June 1998. Suzanne C. Segerstrom, Ph.D., et al.,

> This study polled healthy first-year law students at the beginning of the school year to find out how optimistic they felt about the upcoming year. By the middle of the first semester, the students who had been confident that they would do well had more and better functioning immune cells than the worried students.

2) Research Suggests Optimistic Attitude can Reduce Risk of Heart Disease in Older Men

> For Immediate Release: Wednesday, November 21, 2001
>
> *Boston, MA—Researchers at the Harvard School of Public Health and the Department of Veterans Affairs have linked a more optimistic outlook in older men with a dramatically reduced risk of coronary heart disease (CHD). The study examined the effects of an optimistic versus pessimistic way of explaining events on the incidence of heart attack, angina and fatal CHD among older men; it appears in the*

November/December issue of Psychosomatic Medicine
(www.psychosomatic.org/pm.html)

3) "AGING WITH GRACE: What the Nun Study Teaches Us About Leading Longer, Healthier, and More Meaningful Lives"

> Author: David Snowdon, Ph.D
> Publisher: Bantam
> ISBN: 0553801635

F) Studies on Belief in God reducing stress

1) "The Unique Benefits of Religious Support During Cardiac Bypass Surgery," *The Journal of Pastoral Care* 1999; 53(1): 19-29. Larry VandeCreek, Kenneth Pargament, Timothy Belavich, Brenda Cowell, and Lisa Friedel

    > Studies of patients have found religious coping can enhance recovery from surgery, the researchers noted. A study of more than 230 heart surgery patients at Dartmouth found that six months after surgery, 12 percent of those who rarely or never went to church had died whereas all of those who saw themselves as deeply religious and derived strength or comfort from their faith were still living.

2) "Lack of Social Participation or Religious Strength and Comfort as Risk Factors for Death after Cardiac Surgery in the Elderly." *Psychosomatic Medicine* 1995; 57(1): 5-15. T.E. Oxman, D.H. Freeman, E.D. Manheimer,

    > A study of 232 patients at Dartmouth Medical School found that elderly heart patients were 14 times less

likely to die following surgery if they found strength and comfort in their religious faith and remained socially involved.

3) "The Relationship Between Religious Activities and Blood Pressure in Older Adults." *International Journal of Psychiatry in Medicine* 1998; 28(2): 189-213. H.G. Koenig, et al.

Risk of diastolic hypertension ranked 40 percent lower among people who both attended religious services at least once a week and prayed or studied the Bible at least daily, Duke University researchers found in a study of nearly 4,000 people aged 65 years and older. These findings remained even after taking into account age, gender, race, education and other clinical factors that could affect blood pressure outcomes.

4) "Attendance at Religious Services, Interleukin-6, and Other Biological Parameters of Immune Function in Older Adults." *International Journal of Psychiatry in Medicine* 1997; 27(3): 233-250. Koenig, H.K., et al.

A pioneering study of more than 1,700 older adults from North Carolina conducted by researchers at Duke University Medical Center found that persons who attended church at least once a week were only half as likely as non-attenders to have elevated levels of interleukin-6, an immune system protein involved in a wide variety of age related diseases.

5) "Religiosity and Remission of Depression in Medically Ill Older Patients." *American Journal of Psychiatry* 1998; 155(4): 536-542. H.G. Koenig, L.K. George, B.L Peterson

In a study of 87 depressed older adults hospitalized

with medical illness, researchers at Duke University found the extent to which a patient's religious faith was a central motivating force in their lives, the faster they recovered from depression.

6) "Use of Hospital Services, Religious Attendance, and Religious Affiliation." *Southern Medical Journal* 1998; 91(10): 925-932. H.G. Koenig, D.B. Larson,

> In a study of 542 patients aged 60 or older admitted consecutively to Duke University Medical Center, those who attended religious services weekly or more sliced hospital stays by more than half. People with no religious affiliation spent an average of 25 days in the hospital compared to 11 days for patients affiliated with some religious denomination. Patients who attended religious services weekly or more also were 43 percent less likely to have been hospitalized in the previous year.

7) "Frequent Attendance at Religious Services and Mortality over 28 Years." *American Journal of Public Health* 1997; 87(6): 957-961. W.J. Strawbridge, et al.

> In a study that followed persons from a community for over 28 years, those who attended religious services weekly or more were 25 percent less likely to die than infrequent attenders. Not only were frequent attendees likely to live longer, once they began to attend church they also made healthier lifestyle choices, becoming more apt to quit smoking, to increase exercising, to expand their social support network and to stay married, noted the authors of this study of 5,286 people in Alameda County, California. Thus, these health-enhancing

behaviors of the religiously motivated seemed to contribute, at least in part, to their lower death rates.

8) "Religion and Mortality Among the Community-Dwelling Elderly." *American Journal of Public Health* 1998; 88(10): 1469-1475. D. Oman, D. Reed,

> Attending worship services on a regular basis was an important factor in predicting longevity in a study of 2,025 senior citizens living in Marin County, California. A range of other factors that might have contributed to health and living longer were taken into account, but attending religious services was found to be the most important predictive account.

9) "Religious Involvement and U.S. Adult Mortality." *Demography* 1999; 36(2): 1-13. R.A. Hummer, R.G. Rogers, C. B. Nam C.G. Ellison,

> Attending religious services more than once a week can expand one's life up to seven years and added a potential 14 more years to the life span of African Americans. Tracking a national sample of more than 21,000 U.S. adults, a 1999 study published in *Demography* examined numerous social, economic and health and lifestyle factors, as well as frequency of religious attendance, to see who was most likely to avoid death by any cause during the nine-year follow-up study period. Religious attendance surfaced as a strong predictor for living longer, even when other relevant clinical or social factors were taken into account.

G) C.S. Lewis

To find out more about C.S. Lewis and his works, you may visit the following website: http://cslewis.drzeus.net/

H) Richard Wurmbrand

Pastor Richard Wurmbrand is an evangelical minister who spent fourteen years in Communist imprisonment and torture in his homeland of Romania. He is one of Romania's most widely known Jewish Believer leaders, authors, and educators. In 1945, when the Communists seized Romania and attempted to control the churches for their purposes, Richard Wurmbrand immediately began an effective "underground" ministry to his enslaved people and the invading Russian soldiers. He was eventually arrested in 1948. Richard spent three years in solitary confinement, seeing no one but his Communist torturers.

To find out more about Pastor Wurmbrand, you may visit the following website:
http://home.pacbell.net/andrea/wurmbrandbio.html

Or Contact:
The Voice of the Martyrs
P.O. Box 443
Bartlesville, OK 74005
Phone: 1-800-747-0085 or (918) 337-8015
Fax (918) 338-0189
Website: http://www.persecution.com
Email: thevoice@vom-usa.org

I) John Clayton

Why I Left Atheism by John Clayton

(Reprinted by permission from a booklet)

Of all the lessons that I present concerning the existence of God and of all the material that I try to make available to people to learn about God's existence, the present lesson, "Why I Left Atheism," is the lesson in the series that I frankly do not like to present. I guess none of us like to look back in our lives to a time when we made poor judgments and foolish mistakes—when we took rather really idiotic positions—and admit this, especially to people we are not well acquainted with. I present this lesson, however, because it is my fervent hope and prayer that perhaps by exposing my mistakes and by pointing out the things that were a part of my early life, some who might be following the same paths (to a greater or lesser extent) might not make those same mistakes. Someone once said that nobody is totally useless; if we cannot do anything else, we can at least serve as a bad example. That is sort of my situation. I am hoping that by presenting these materials and telling you something about my early life, some of you may be able to recognize the lack of wisdom and perhaps the poor judgment that is involved in rejecting God and living a life that demonstrates such a rejection.

Most of the time when I speak to religious groups or to people who believe in God, someone will ask me somewhat incredulously, "Well, were you really an atheist? Did you really not believe in God?" I want to start by asserting that the answer to that question is a very affirmative "Yes." At one time in my life, I was totally and firmly convicted that there was no such thing as God and that anybody who believed in God was silly, superstitious, ignorant, and had simply not looked at the evidence. I felt that believers in God were uneducated and were just following traditions, superstitions, and things that really made no sense to a person who was aware of what was going on around them. Of course, that kind of life and conviction led me to do and say things and to be something that was really very unpleasant. I lived a life that was immoral and which reflected a lack of belief in God. I lived in a way that was very self-centered and that satisfied my own pleasures and desires regardless of whether or not other people were hurt in the process of what I was doing. In the process of doing this, I did a lot of things that affected me through my whole life. It is because of this that I present these materials hoping that perhaps some of you will not make the mistakes and suffer the consequences that I have suffered. I cannot clearly remember all of the events that took place or the proper sequence of events because I was not taking notes. I never expected that I would be trying to recall these things, much less tell someone else about them. Still, I can recall in a general way much of what happened, and I am very sure of the concepts. It is the concepts that will be most useful to you.

I guess the reason that I was an atheist is the same reason that many of you are believers in God if you are. That was because I had been indoctrinated in that particular persuasion. My background, the variables that were exposed to me as a child, led me very strongly in that direction. Just as many of you believe in God because your parents believe in God and because they instilled this belief in you, I also questioned, challenged, and rejected God because that was the kind of indoctrination that I received as a child. I can remember my mother saying to me as a child something like, "Do you really believe there is an old man, floating around in the sky, blasting things into existence here upon the earth? Do you really believe that crummy looking structure on the corner could be something beautiful called 'the church?' Do your really believe that there is a hole in the ground that I am going to be thrown into and burned eternally if I do not live just the way some preacher thinks I ought to?" Of course, I could not conceive of these things as a child and did not know enough to realize they are not what the Bible teaches. Consequently, I came to believe that anybody who believed in God was just silly, superstitious, ignorant and unlearned. You may wonder how it would be possible for a person coming out of this type of background and kind of learning situation to come to be a strong believer in God today, devoting his life to trying to help people to understand that there is a God in heaven and that the Bible is His literal and verbally inspired Word.

My high school career was one in which I grew quite rapidly academically, I enjoyed science and decided that I wanted to be a scientist of some kind. I entered Indiana University majoring in the field of physical science. It was actually at this point that one of the great changes that occurred in my life took place. I enrolled in a course in astronomy at the feet of one of the great astronomers of our day. In that particular course, we were studying the problem of origins—the creation of matter from nothing. As we discussed this particular subject, we went into all those theories that are in that particular material. We talked about the big-bang theory, the quasistatal theory, the continuous generation theory, the planetessimal theory, etc.

When we got to the conclusion of that discussion, I asked the professor which of the particular theories was the one that is most acceptable and that satisfactorily explains the creation of matter from nothing. He leaned over the desk and looked me straight in the eye and said, "Young man, you need to learn to ask intelligent questions." That rather upset me. I did not appreciate that and I said, "Well, what do you mean?" He said, "This is not a question that a scientist tries to answer. This is a question for the philosopher or theologian, but this in not something that falls into the realm of science." In today's discussions of black holes and parallel universe things have not changed. The basic question of the creation of matter/energy from absolutely nothing is not an area that can be scientifically explored. I was very disturbed by that answer. I had always felt that science could ultimately answer all the questions that man had—that there was nothing that science could not eventually take care of as far as what man might challenge and want to know about. Yet this learned man, and expert in his field, said that this was an area that the scientist should not even try to answer—

that it was totally beyond the capacity of science to explain and explore.

Not too long after that, I enrolled in a course in biology at the feet of one of the great primitive life scientists in the country. As we discussed the initial beginning of life upon the earth in that class, we talked about the synthesis of various primitive chemical materials such as deoxyribonucleic acid (DNA). As we discussed this, I once again asked a question related to the one that I had asked previously. I asked this professor what the process was by which the original life—the original living cells upon the earth—came into existence. How did the structure or generation of DNA occur? Once again, this man said, "Young man, that is not a question that falls within the realm of science." In today's world we understand more about biochemical processes, but we cannot answer how in the environment of the primitive earth these processes came into operation. I guess what was happening to me was the same thing that Lord Kelvin, a very famous British scientist, described in his writings when he made the statement, "If you study science deep enough and long enough it will force you to believe in God." That is what happened to me. I began to realize that science had its limitations—that science, in fact, strongly pointed to other explanations than natural ones to certain questions.

It was about this time when another thing happened in my life and that was that a woman entered it. A lot of things begin with women (some things end with them, too). In this particular case, this young lady was by all means the most bullheaded, stubborn, cast-iron willed individual I had ever met in all my life. I can make those statements because some six years later I married her. This was the first girl I ever met that I felt I could respect. Sometimes you will hear preachers who know absolutely nothing about what they are talking about from the role of experience make statements such as, "If you hold on to your virtues and maintain your moral standards, a man will respect you more." Let me tell you, as one who his lived on the other side of the fence and has thought as one who is alienated form how God thinks, that statement is true. I will guarantee you that I never thought seriously about marrying anyone until I met this girl who I could respect—who really stood for something. Not only did she stand for something morally, she believed in God and read her Bible. Though she could not answer all my questions, she kept going back to the Bible. I also learned quickly not to let her know what I was really like morally. I knew if she really knew that, she would have nothing to do with me. I did not seem to be able to break her faith as I had been able to do with other people and the thing that happened was that as a result of her stubbornness and refusal to reject the Bible, she forced me to read the Bible.

I read the Bible through from cover to cover four times during my sophomore year in college for the explicit purpose of finding scientific contradictions in it. By that, I mean statements in the Bible that were false that I could throw back at her to show her how ridiculous it was to believe in God. I had even decided to write a book called *All the Stupidity of the Bible.* Something amazing happened as I did this. As I considered and thought about these things, I found that I could not find a contradiction—to find some kind of scientific inaccuracy in the Bible. I just simply was not able to do it. I gave up writing the book because of lack of material! It is amazing to me that as I talk to people, I find many who claim to be Christians and who perhaps claim to have been Christians for many years who have not read the Bible through cover to cover once. I find it hard to believe that they believe in God very much if they do not even what to know what He has to say.

As I read the Bible through again and again, I began to realize that all the things I had been told about God and religion were not what the Bible said. They may have been what organized religion said or what some men taught, but not what the Bible itself said. For example, the Bible did not say that God was an old man floating around in the sky, blasting things into existence here upon the earth. The Bible said, "God *is* a spirit..." (John 4:24) and that God in not flesh and blood. Jesus made the statement, "... for flesh and blood hath not revealed *it* unto thee, but my Father which is in heaven." (Matthew 16:17). There are many people who do not understand this. A Russian astronaut once made the statement, "See, I told you there was no God; I didn't see him when I was in orbit." The question might be, "What was he looking for?" I began to recognize that God was not an old man in the sky. I had an anthropology professor not too long ago who made the statement in all dead seriousness, "We all know what God is; He is an old man with a long white beard and big flowing robes." I am sure that this was his concept of "god." I began to recognize that this was not the biblical concept of God.

I began to recognize that the Christian life was not an altruistic life. I had been told by several people as a child that if you ever become a Christian, you cannot ever be happy, you cannot ever own anything, and you have to walk around with a long sad face with your chin dragging the ground. Yet when I read the Bible, I read statements like, "So ought men to love their wives as their own bodies. He that loveth his wife loveth himself. For no man ever yet hated his own flesh; but nourisheth and cherisheth it..." (Ephesians 5:28-29). I read about the Ethiopian eunuch who went on his way *rejoicing* because he had found Jesus Christ and the happiness that went with that acceptance of Jesus in his life. I have had many problems come into my life, but all I have to do is to look back at how miserable life was without Christ and I can realize that life, as it is now with Jesus, is beautiful in comparison.

I began to recognize that the Church was not a building. I can remember that when we lived in Alabama, there was a meeting place of some religious group just down the street from us. My mother used to point to that as we drove or walked by and say, "Look at that. How could anybody believe in God when the Church looks like that." I realized that the Bible did not teach that the Church is such a structure. I Corinthians 3:16 makes the statement, "Know ye not that ye are the temple of God . . ." As an atheist, I recognized that you could meet on the moon, in a submarine, out in the desert, or any place else and still be the Church. The Church was not a building. What a tragedy it is that so many today have invested enormous amounts of money in edifices and buildings, while other human beings have gone hungry nearby.

I began to recognize that hypocrisy was not confined to religion. I had the idea that every hypocrite in the world sat in a pew on Sunday morning, and thus that everybody who was not sitting in a pew was not a hypocrite. I remember the lesson I learned on this. There was a young man who would sit elbow to elbow with me arguing against the religionist from time-to-time. He was in the hospital once with a very serious ailment. I went up to visit him and as I opened the hospital door, I saw him down on his knees praying to God. I stood at the door of that hospital room screaming at him, "You hypocrite—you dirty hypocrite!" until I was escorted out of the hospital. It slowly began to dawn on me that hypocrisy is a function of humanity, not religion. You deal with hypocrites at the grocery store, at the filling station, on the job, at school, and at the golf course (maybe more there than anywhere else). You do not quit buying groceries because the grocer says one thing and does another. You do not quit your job because your employers tell you to do something that they themselves would not touch with a ten-foot pole. You do not deprive yourself or your child of a good education because a teacher teaches one thing and lives something else. You do not quit playing golf because your buddy takes a stroke in the rough and does not count it when he thinks you did not see it. Sure there is hypocrisy in the Church, because there are human beings in the Church, and as long as you deal with human beings, you are going to deal with hypocrisy. Do you want to get away from hypocrisy? Dig a 20-foot hole in your back yard, jump in, let someone cover you with dirt, and even *then* you are going to be sitting down there in the bottom of that hole with one hypocrite. There is not a one of us breathing air that is as consistent as we ought to be, but the person who says, "I'm not going to be a Christian! I'm not going to serve God! I'm not going to get involved in the work of the Church because there are hypocrites in the Church," is just logically inconsistent! WE do not use that kind of thinking anywhere else in our lives. How can we do it in our relationship to God? There were many, many misconceptions that I had to get rid of to really understand what the Bible really teaches.

Another thing that I think needs to be mentioned here as we discuss some of the things that led me to believe in God were things that had to do with my happiness. I remember that as a young person, I had what would be an ideal home by worldly standards. My parents were marvelous people; there was no divorce, unfaithfulness, or neglect in my family. WE did things as a family. WE enjoyed each other, yet I ran away from home. I was rebellious and antagonistic. As I look back at God's Word today, I can see why these things happened. In Colossians 3:20, for example, the Bible says, "Children, obey *your* parents in all things: for this is well-pleasing unto the Lord." Obedience was not a characteristic of John Clayton as a young man. Living in Bloomington, Indiana, Indianapolis was known as the *party town*, and if I wanted to go to Indianapolis, I went. When my mother said she did not want me to go, I disconnected the speedometer and went. I did anything and everything I wanted to do. After all, there was no God. All my parents were doing was restricting my fun and enjoyment in life; why should I obey them? I lived a life that was totally antagonistic to everything that my parents stood for. It is amazing to me today that some parents who do not believe in God and demonstrate this lack of belief to their children by what they say or the way they live wonder why their children will not obey them. Why should they? They have removed the only source of authority that they have, and no child is going to obey a parent who has destroyed that source of authority. I am convinced that much of our law and order problems center around this very question.

Recently, I was talking to a young man in Michigan who had been a participant in some of the riots at the University of Michigan. He made the statement to me that he had done these things and I asked him why he had not obeyed the law. He said, "What law?" and I said, "The law of the land—the law that God has instituted." He looked at me and laughed and said, "Man, I don't believe in God." I do not believe we can have law and order when we remove the source of the authority to that law and order. Certainly, my rebelliousness and failure to obey my parents brought a great deal of unpleasantness and misery not only into my life, but into theirs. The very next verse in Colossians 3 contains another statement that I think had a great deal to do with my unhappiness and rebelliousness as a child. The statement is made, "Fathers provoke not your children *to anger*, lest they be discouraged." My parents had a tradition when I was a young man—a tradition they called *the cocktail hour*. I have never seen my parents drunk, but they would drink a few martinis and my mother would ask me questions that ordinarily she would not have asked. I remember, for instance, she would sometimes ask, "What did you do with the girl you took out last night?" That was the last thing I was going to tell my mother, so I learned to look her right straight in the eye and lie. I could lie to her or anybody else without batting an eyelash. I conditioned myself to do things that were wrong. I conditioned myself to steal. I remember the first time that I stole something. It was a box of raisins from the IGA store. I felt so badly that I took it back and apologized. Sometime later, I stole a comic book from a drug store; I took it back, but I did not apologize. Six months from then, I was stealing almost anything I could get my hands on, not because I needed it, but because it was fun—it was a challenge. I even went so far as to be caught stealing money from my parents. That brings me to the next point, which is certainly another thing that had to do with my happiness.

When I read passages in the Bible like the 53rd Psalm, for instance, I sometimes almost feel like God is describing John Clayton some years ago. Psalm 53:1-3 says:

> The fool hath said in his heart, "*There* is no God." Corrupt are they, and have done abominable iniquity: *there is* none that doeth good. God looked down from heaven upon the children of men, to see if there were *any* that did understand, that did seek God. Every one of them is gone back: they are altogether become filthy; *there is* none that doeth good, no, not one.

Another statement, made by Solomon in Ecclesiastes 1:2-3, 14, says:

> Vanity of vanities, saith the Preacher, vanity of vanities; all *is* vanity. What profit hath a man of all his labour which he taketh under the sun? . . . I have seen all the works that are done under the sun; and, behold, all *is* vanity and vexation of spirit.

I have tried almost everything you can imagine to find pleasure and happiness. I will not try to tell you that I did not find pleasure using my own system of following my own desires, but I can guarantee you that I did not find happiness. I tried every conceivable thing you can think of. I tried all kinds of things—things that were immoral, that were wrong, that hurt other people, and things that I would not even want to describe. I did those things because I was trying to find pleasure and happiness and, as I say, I found pleasure sometimes. However, I never went to bed at night satisfied or happy with my life and enjoying my living. I never got up in the morning looking forward to a new day. Life was just one long chain of misery.

Judge Roy Moore of Lawton, Oklahoma, who deals with the legal problems precipitated by the presence of For Sill in that area, once made the statement to me, "I've never seen a young man on drugs live more than seven years without taking his life." You may not be able to understand that, but I have sat on the edge of my bed with a .22 caliber rifle between my legs, trying to have enough guts to pull the trigger. I bottomed out that low; I got that emotionally disturbed and upset with my desire and attempt to find happiness. Please listen to me and profit by what I am saying. You can try every conceivable thing that this world has to offer. You can try sex, drugs, alcohol, stealing, and all kinds of things in a desperate attempt to find happiness. I can testify from experience that you may find pleasure, but you will not find happiness. I can go back to Bloomington today and meet people who refuse to believe that I have changed my life—people that I hurt and who knew the kind of life I lived. The reason that I think many things happen with young people today is because they try to find happiness living their own way. It simply does not work. Have you ever wondered why it is that when a person gets clean on drugs, gets rid of the problem of alcohol or conquers some of the problems like the ones I had, that the person always seems to get involved in some religious cause, halfway house or something like that? Why is that? I can tell you from my own experience that we have learned that the only place you find happiness is in using God's system—in following God's way. Perhaps people that have lived without God appreciate so much more than people that have grown up in religious structures—what you have in the Church. You do not find happiness living your own system, but only in living God's way and in being a part of God's system.

As perhaps you are beginning to realize as we get into this discussion more thoroughly, there were a variety of things that led me to believe in God. One other thing that I think ought to be mentioned is the fact that I entered a period of military service about this time. For the first time in my life, I came in contact with death. I began to think about the reasonableness of death as I looked at it as an atheist. Perhaps a more accurate way to describe this was the way that I had to look at life because of death. As an atheist, I realized that I had to look at life with all of its problems, difficulties, and terrible things that I experienced as the best thing that I could ever look forward to. Yet I realized that as a Christian, I would be able to look at life with all of its joys, beauties, and wonderful things that we all enjoy as the absolute worst that I was ever going to have to experience. Yet from a philosophical point, I began to realize that Christianity offered a great deal in this particular area. I did not get scared into believing in God, but I think this area together with all these other things helped to make me realize that there really was quite a change in my understanding of what Christianity and God are all about. I began to recognize that perhaps there were some things about the Church and what it had to offer that were important to me.

About this time in my life, I decided that other religious systems *might* be as good as the Bible. To check them out, I began reading the Vedas, Koran, Sayings of Buddha, writings of Bahaullah and Zoroaster and found that other religions taught many things I could not accept. There were teachings in their writings concerning what life was like after this life that were unrewarding and unrealistic and there were descriptions of God that were illogical and inconsistent. There were also many scientific inaccuracies in their works. There were many teachings about life and how to live it that were not workable. This included the role and position of women in the Koran, the Holy War concept of Mohammed, the pantheism of nearly all other systems, reincarnation, idol worship, polygamy, and a myriad of ideas which I had expected to find in the Bible, but did not. I began to realize that nothing matched the Bible's system of life. Only in the Bible could I see statements which would stand in the face of the scientific facts that I knew to be true and only the Bible offered a system of life that I felt was reasonable and consistent. I decided that if I ever came to believe in God, it would be a belief based upon the Bible.

The next question was that if I ever became a believer in God, which of all the religious organizations claiming to be Christianity would be the correct one. I recognized that I did not want to be a part of all these traditional religious bodies that taught the error that I had been taught and had believed in my early years, so I started visiting the various religious organizations in southern Indiana at that time. I visited almost every religious organization that I could get into, to try and see what they taught, to see if they followed the Bible and if they understood what the Bible had to say or if they followed men's theologies. My experience was that as I went from one to another, each of them taught something that was not in the Bible. They honored some men above other men, they taught that unreligious writings were equivalent to the Bible and they did not follow the Bible literally and verbally. I had had enough of religious confusion and error. I did not want any more of that sort of thing, so I continued looking. In a real sense, I guess you could say I am still looking—I am still trying to find that true Church. I did find the religious group that seemed to me to follow the Bible very closely. In Bloomington, there was a group of people who met on the corner of 4th and Lincoln streets. They were called the *Church of Christ*. These people still did not totally follow what I understood to be the biblical system. My challenge today to young people who are Christians would be to do a job of totally restoring New Testament

Christianity. This group did have the doctrine of Christianity pretty well restored as I understood it. I recognized that passages like 1 Peter 3:21 ("The like figure whereunto *even* baptism doth also now save us . . .) had to be interpreted as meaning what it said, and this group did interpret that in a way that I felt was consistent with that passage. This group did interpret Acts 2:38 (" . . . be baptized every one of you in the name of Jesus Christ for the remission of sins . . ." in a way that I felt was consistent and they did reject men as their source of authority.

As a matter of fact, I remember hearing one of the first lessons that I ever heard in that building preached by a man by the name of Raymond Muncy. Mr. Muncy said something about, "Now, don't you ever listen to anything any preacher says," and I said amen to that. He went on and talked about how we should not rely upon man and I want to tell you hear and now that you should never believe anything any preacher says. Do not ever listen to any preacher, under any circumstance, unless you can find for yourself in the Bible that what that man says is consistent with God's Word. This is, in essence, what Mr. Muncy was saying and I was very impressed by it, but that group of people did not give as they were prospered. Yes, they worshipped according to God's format, but they did not give as they were prospered. They were not involved in teaching their neighbors about Jesus Christ. There was a very small percentage who were active in the work and they certainly did not manifest the kind of love and appreciation for each other that I understood the Bible to teach. The generation before you has restored the doctrine of Christianity—I believe that. However, they have yet to restore the spirit of New Testament Christianity and that is your challenge. Restore the spirit of New Testament Christianity—the love and the concern for the souls of others that the early Church had. I recognized that the Church of Christ was the closest thing that I had seen to what the Bible taught. I determined that if I ever became a Christian, I would become a member of this group—a group that was trying to follow the Bible literally and verbally, that would not accept the teachings of men and would not try to be influenced by the traditions of the past.

I guess the real straw that broke the camel's back occurred some six months later. I was enrolled in my first geology course at Indiana University. The professor was a brilliant, well-known atheist. On the first day of class, in response to a discussion, he made a statement something like, "I'm going to show you that the Bible is a bunch of garbage," and I thought, "Now this is going to be great," because I was getting concerned. I was still saying that I was an atheist to those who knew me well. I was still rejecting God and holding on tenaciously to my lack of belief. It is hard to change a life that has gone a certain direction for years and all of a sudden make it go another direction and I was not ready for that. I thought this man was going to be able to provide me with some arguments that would finally defeat this girl that I had been dating all these years. She was a Christian—although perhaps not as strong as she might have been. I was going to show her that this religion stuff was really a lot of bunk and I was even convinced that I might even be able to show Ray Muncy that belief in God was not realistic. Mr. Muncy was a man who had great patience and knowledge, but he had not been given much of an opportunity to convince or teach me much of anything.

The professor started the class out by showing us the various methods of dating rocks and other parts of the creation. He then asserted that everyone knew that the Bible said the earth was 6,000 years old. I asked where it said that. He replied that he believed it was in Genesis the 52nd chapter. I started looking, not knowing much about the Bible, to Genesis 40, 49, Genesis 50, Exodus 1—I said, "Wait a minute; Genesis only has 50 chapters." He sputtered around a few minutes, but he never did find that passage. Of course, the Bible does not say the earth is 6,000 years old. The Bible is totally silent on the age of the earth and I realized that. This man made the statement that the Bible says that God created two cocker spaniels, two English terriers and two German shepherds. We all had a good laugh when we figured out how big the Ark would have to be to hold the 20 million groupings of this kind. Once again, I asked where the word *kind* was defined in that way. It did not seem to me that the word *kind* meant that. We looked at it and he finally said he guessed that maybe it did not. 1 Corinthians 15:39 is the only definition of the word *kind* and that is a very broad definition (All flesh is not the same flesh: but *there is* one *kind* of flesh of men, another flesh of beasts, another fishes, *and* another of birds.) Genesis 1 uses the same terminology and the same breakdown as 1 Corinthians 15. To make a very, very long story fairly short, when I turned in my final exam the last day of class, I said to this learned professor, "Sir, you have not really shown me any contradiction between what we have studied in this course and in what the bible has to teach." He jerked my paper away from me and said, "Well, I guess if you really study it, there is no contradiction." I was shocked! I was appalled! Here was a man who had a Ph.D. and was leading atheist, yet he could not answer my silly questions, from an ignorant college junior who was on his side. I remember that February day very clearly. I walked back to my room in the dormitory in a state of shock. I could not believe what had happened. I got to my room about 11:00 and sat on my bed thinking what a stupid, ignorant fool I had been. I had rejected God; I had been dishonest. I had actually been stupid in my response to the evidence available to me. I did not like people who refuse to look at the evidence and draw intelligent conclusions, I did not like people who could not break free of their parents' thinking and do their own thinking. I had always accused the religionist of doing this, yet I recognized that I had been guilty of the same thing. I had refused to be honest—to look at the evidence. I had refused to make comparative choices based upon what was available to me. I was miserable.

Supper time came and I was sitting there. My roommate came in and said, "Are you ready to eat?" I said, "No, I'm not hungry." He said, "Are you sick?" I said, "Yes, I'm sick of me!!! I'm sick of being selfish, I'm sick of using people, I'm sick of being dishonest, I'm sick . . ." I was still telling him what I was sick about as he left for supper. At the time, I did not understand what was happening, but I do now! That is what repentance is all about—to get sick of a selfish, egotistical, destructive life and turn to God's way—to turn to a life that has value, meaning, and direction. My roommate went on to eat and I just sat there determined that I had to do something. I could no longer sit back and be dishonest and continue to refuse to accept the obvious evidence that was available to me. About 6:30, I got up and started walking toward the building where the Church of Christ met on Wednesday nights. The invitation was extended at the Church of Christ that evening for anyone who wished to accept Christ and come forward. I went forward, understanding that I now believed totally and completely in God. I recognized that I needed to start a new life and be willing to tell people that I accepted the existence of God and believed that Jesus is His Son. I also realized that I was totally and completely lost in my sins and that I needed to be baptized to have forgiveness (as the Bible commanded). I started down the aisle that night and Raymond Muncy went into a mild state of shock. I remember the expression on his face. I do not think he believed that the power of God could ever reach a man as divorced as I was from anything good, decent and godly. I was baptized into Christ that evening fro the remission of my sins, as I understood the Bible to teach. To show you how far I was from God, I called this girl I had been dating for some six years at that time. I said, "Phyllis, I've become a Christian!" She said, "I don't believe you. You quit lying to me." I had to have the preacher's wife talk to her to convince her that I had, in fact, become a Christian. There are people today who still do not believe it—that the power of God could change a man that was as divorced and alienated from God as I was—but I want to tell you that in many respects, this is just the beginning of this story. God promised His help to those who are His followers. Having a close personal relationship to God and to other followers enable us to conquer enormous problems and do things we could not possibly do on our own. (see Philippians 4:13).

I had a lot to overcome. I could not talk without swearing. You could not go to the preacher's house and say pass the @$%& potatoes. I had to learn a new way of talking, a new way of living, a new set of values and a new morality, because I had lived in opposition to God. I asked God's help in these things and I found I was able to overcome things I had never been able to overcome before. I have a whole new set of problems—a whole new set of things that I have to work on—but the problems I have today are nothing like the problems I had in the past. If anyone had told me twenty years ago that I would be openly using my limited abilities to publicly convict disbelievers of God's reality, I would have thought they were insane. Nonetheless, God has blessed my feeble efforts in spectacular ways—totally beyond anything I could have ever done.

I want to close this lesson by asking you a very simple question—a question that you need to answer for yourself and that each person needs to answer I suppose nearly every day. Are you an atheist (not perhaps as man would define it, but as God defines it)? Are you an atheist? Oh, I realize you may not be the kind of atheist that I was. Perhaps you are not immoral or hurting people or dishonest or doing the kinds of things that I did. I am thankful that you are not, but do you realize the way Jesus view an atheist? Matthew 12:30 says, **"He that is not with me is against me; and he that gathereth not with me scattereth abroad."** What is He saying? He is saying that you are either for God or you are against God. You are either an atheist or a Christian; you cannot be both. I can understand how a man can be an atheist. I have been an atheist a good part of my life. As an atheist, I believed (and still believe) that my life was consistent, reasonable and defendable.

For a few years now, I have been trying to live what I understand to be the Christian way of life. Once again, I believe my life is consistent, reasonable, and defendable with what I believe, but I will never understand (and if you understand, I wish you would explain it to me) how a man or a woman or a boy or a girl can say, "Yes, I believe in God. Yes, I understand that the Bible is God's Word," and then not do everything and anything within their power to make sure their lives conform to that which God teaches. That is not consistent, not reasonable, and not defendable, yet I am sure there are many people who know that their life is not consistent with God's way of living. Jesus said, "He that is not with me is against me; and he that gathereth not with me scattereth abroad." Are you for Christ? Are you working for Christ? Is your live radiating the kind of living that Jesus taught? Are you really a Christian or are you and atheist? There is no middle ground. It is my hope that by revealing to you the kind of person I have been and the mistakes I have made, you have realized that God is the only way. It is my prayer that you have realized that there is nothing that can be a part of your life that God cannot help you overcome and that you also realize that there is no better time than right now to begin the Christian way of living. Will you not give yourself to God and live Christ's Way? If you do not know a person or group of people in your community following the Lord, write me and I will try to help you.

—End of Testimony—
Contact Information:

Office Address:
Does God Exist?
718 E. Donmoyer Ave.,
South Bend, IN 46614-1999
Home Address:
John Clayton
1555 Echo Valley Dr.
Niles, MI 49120
E-mail: *jncdge@aol.com*
Website: *http://www.doesgodexist.org*

J) Dr. Hugh Ross

For Dr. Ross's testimony, please visit the following website:
Website: *http://www.reasons.org*

For a catalog of materials on subjects pertaining to faith, science, and the Bible please contact:
Reasons to Believe
P.O. Box 5978
Pasadena, CA 91117
Phone: 1-800-482-7836 or (626) 335-1480

K) Exercise Resources to get your shape back after delivering a baby

The New Mother's Body Book
Author: Jacqueline Shannon, Designed by Neysa Whiteman
Publisher: Contemporary Books, Incorporated, April 1994, ISBN: 0809237954

Positive Parenting Fitness: A Total Approach to Caring for the Physical and Emotional Needs of Your New Family
Author: Sylvia Llein Olkin Preface by Pamela Shrock
Publisher: Avery Publishing Group, Inc., November 1991, ISBN: 0895294818

Primetime Pregnancy: The Proven Program for Staying in Shape Before and After Your Baby Is Born
Author: Kathy Kaehler, Cynthia Tivers
Publisher: NTC Publishing Group, November 1997, ISBN: 0809230720

From Baby to Bikini: Keep Your Muscles Toned Safely during Pregnancy and Flatten Your Abdominals Fast after You Have Your Baby
Author: Greg Waggoner, Doug Stumpf
Publisher: Warner Books, Incorporated. April 1999, ISBN: 0446673986

Appendix 4

Contact Information

A) Al-Anon:

Phone: 888-4AL-ANON (888-425-2666)
E-mail: *WSO@al-anon.org*
Website: *http://www.al-anon.alateen.org/*

B) Alcoholics Anonymous:

World Services, Inc.
Street address:
Alcoholics Anonymous
475 Riverside Dr.
11th Floor
New York, NY 10115

Mailing Address:
Alcoholics Anonymous
Grand Central Station
P.O. Box 495
New York, NY 10163

Website: *http://www.alcoholics-anonymous.org/*

C) Beauty Consultants:

1) Paula Begoun
   The Cosmetics Cop
   13075 Gateway Drive, Suite 160
   Seattle, WA 98168
   Phone: (800) 831-4088 (From the U.S. and Canada) or (206) 444-1622
   Fax: (206) 444-1625
   E-mail: *custserv@cosmeticscop.com*
   Website: *http://www.cosmeticscop.com/*

2) Beautydebut.com
   http://www.galaxymall.com/beauty/beautydebut/index.html

3) Mary Kay Cosmetics
   To find a Beauty Consultant in your area
   Call: 1-800-Mary Kay
   (1-800-627-9529)
   Or write to:
   Mary Kay, Inc.
   P.O. Box 799045
   Dallas, Texas 75379-9045

D) Bible Resources:

1) Institute for Biblical and Scientific Studies
   http://www.bibleandscience.com

2) The Bible Gateway
   http://bible.gospelcom.net/bible?

3) 21 Century Christian
   http://www.21stcc.com/

4) Bible Crosswalk
   http://bible.crosswalk.com/

5) Blue Letter Bible
   http://www.blueletterbible.org/

E) Christian Counseling:

1) Christian Counseling Ministries
   P.O. Box 789
   Buena Vista, CO 81211

   Phone: (719) 395-6423
   Fax: (719) 395-6696
   E-mail: icmco@amigo.net
   Website: *http://www.intensivecounseling.org/*

2) Barnabus Christian Counseling Network
   Website: *http://www.barnabus.com/*

3) Christian Counseling and Educational Foundation
   1803 E. Willow Grove Ave.
   Glenside, PA 19038

   Phone: 215-884-7676
   Fax: 215-884-9435
   E-mail: *CCEFMail@aol.com*
   Website: *http://www.ccef.org/*

4) Christian Counseling Center Referral Network
   Website: *http://www.hope-healing.com/*

F) Color Consulting:

Determining Personal Colors

Susan Wright, Extension Clothing and
Textiles Specialist
College of Agriculture and Home
Economics
New Mexico State University

Website: *http://www.cahe.nmsu.edu/pubs/_c/c-315.html*

G) Eating Disorders:

National Eating Disorders Association
603 Stewart Street, Suite 803
Seattle, WA 98101
Phone: (206) 382-3587
Business Fax: (206) 829-8501
(800) 931-2237 toll-free information and referral hotline or call our business line at ext. 18.
E-mail: *info@NationalEatingDisorders.org*
Website: *http://www.NationalEatingDisorders.org*

H) Health Education:

1) Reality Zone
   PO Box 4646
   Thousand Oaks, CA 91359
   Phone: (800) 595-6596
   E-mail: *webmaster@realityzone.com*
   Website: *http://www.realityzone.com/*

2) Tetrahedron Publishing Group
   206 North 4th Avenue, Suite 147
   Sandpoint, ID 83864
   Phone: 1-888-508-4787 or 208-265-2575
   Fax: 208-265-2775

      E-mail: *tetra@tetrahedron.org*
      Website: *http://www.tetrahedron.org/*

3) The Cancer Cure Foundation
   Newbury Park, California
   (800) 282-2873
   Website: *http://www.cancure.org*

4) Center for Holistic Life Extension
   Mailing address: 482 W. San Ysidro Blvd. Suite 1365
   San Ysidro, California 92173
   Phone: (800) 664-8660
   Website: *http://www.extendlife.com/daily.html*

I) Overeaters Anonymous:

      World Service Office (WSO)
      6075 Zenith Ct. NE
      Rio Rancho, NM 87124
      Phone: 505-891-2664
      Fax: 505-891-4320
      E-mail: *info@overeatersanonymous.org*
      Website: *http://www.Overeatersanonymous.org*

J) Questions for the Author:

      E-mail J.J. at: *questions4jj@mail2america.com*

K) Self-Improvement:

1) Circle "A" Ministries
   9785 Edgerton
   Rockford, Michigan 49341

Phone (616) 866-9979
Contact Person: Skip Ross

2) Dale Carnegie
Look up "Dale Carnegie" in the white pages of your local phone book
Website: *www.dalecarnegie.com*

3) Assertiveness training classes—to find classes in your area, do a search on the internet for "Assertiveness training classes" or check with a community college in your area.

4) Life Success Systems
The Praxis Group
939 Lawrence Avenue East, Box 47611
Toronto, Ontario M3C 3S7

Phone: (416) 449-9958,
(800) 576-6416
Fax: (416) 449-9882
Contact Person: Mark Low
E-mail: *mlow@istar.ca*
Website: *http://www.3percentclub.com*

L) Volunteer Organizations/Service Clubs:

1) Girl Scouts of the USA
420 Fifth Avenue
New York, New York 10018-2798
Phone: (800) GSUSA 4 U [(800) 478-7248] or
(212) 852-8000
Website: *http://www.girlscouts.org/*

2) Camp Fire USA National Headquarters
4601 Madison Avenue

Kansas City, Missouri 64112-1278
Telephone: (816) 756-1950
Fax: (816) 756-0258
Marketing and Communications Fax: (816) 756-2650
E-mail: *info@campfireusa.org*
Website: *http://www.campfire.org/*

3) Lions Club International Headquarters
300 W. 22nd Street
Oak Brook, IL 60523

Phone: (630) 571-5466
Website: *http://www.lionsclubs.org/*

4) BPO Elks of the USA
2750 N. Lakeview Avenue
Chicago, IL 60614-1889

Phone: (773) 755-4700
FAX: (773) 755-4790
Website: *http://www.elks.org/default.cfm*

5) Rotary International
One Rotary Center
1560 Sherman Ave.
Evanston, IL 60201, USA
Phone: 847-866-3000
Fax: 847-328-8554 or 847-328-8281
Website: *http://www.rotary.org/*

6) Soroptimist
Two Penn Center Plaza, Suite 1000
Philadelphia, PA 19102

Phone: (215) 557-9300
Fax: (215) 568-5200

Toll-free hotline: (800) 942-4629
General E-mail: *siahq@soroptimist.org*
Website: *http://www.soroptimist.org/*

M) Women's Shelter:

P. O. Box 1207
Arlington, Texas 76004

The Women's Shelter 24-Hour Hotline (817) 460-5566
National Domestic Violence Hotline 1-800-799-SAFE
(1-800-799-7233)
E-mail: *womensshelter@hotmail.com*
Website: *http://www.womensshelter.org/*

N) Woman's Intimacy Products:

Alura, Website:
http://www.mylexxus.com
Woman's Response Cream, Website:
http://www.findsupplements.com

Appendix 5

Credits

A) Author Unknown

B) Jim Barksdale, Member, Board of Directors, America Online

C) *The Jack Bull*
   Medium: Movie
   Genre: Western
   Director: John Badham
   Cast: John Cusack, John Goodman, L. Q. Jones, Miranda Otto, John Savage,
   John C. McGinley
   Year: 1999

D) Jimi Hendrix

E) Alexander Hamilton

F) "Get Over It!"
   Medium: Song
   Composers: Don Henley and Glenn Frey
   Performed by: Eagles
   Album: Hell Freezes Over
   Year: 1994

G) Robert Burton (1577-1640)
Anatomy of Melancholy

H) Deceived
Medium: Movie
Genre: Mystery/Thriller/Psychodrama
Director: Damian Harris
Cast: Tom Irwin, Goldie Hawn, Amy, Wright, Kate Reid, Beatrice Straight
Year: 1991

I) Shakespeare, *The Merchant of Venice*

J) John Milton, *Paradise Lost*

K) *Runaway Bride*
Medium: Movie
Genre: Romantic Comedy
Director: Garry Marshall
Cast: Julia Roberts, Richard Gere, Joan Cusack, Hector Elizondo, Rita Wilson, Paul Dooley
Year: 1999

L) Harry Truman

M) *Airplane*
Medium: Movie
Genre: Comedy
Directors: Jim Abrahams, David Zucker, and Jerry Zucker
Cast: Robert Hays, Julie Hagerty, Lloyd Bridges, Leslie Nielsen, Peter Graves, Robert Stack, Kareem Abdul-Jabbar, Lorna Patterson, Stephen Stucker, Jim Abrahams, Frank Ashmore, Jonathan Banks, Craig Berenson, Barbara Billingsley, Lee Bryant
Year: 1980

N) *Naked Gun*
   Medium: Movie
   Genre: Comedy
   Director: David Zucker
   Cast: Leslie Nielsen, O.J. Simpson, Priscilla Presley, George Kennedy, Ricardo Montalban
   Year: 1988

O) "Breaking up is hard to do" quote from the song "Breaking Up Is Hard To Do"
   Medium: Song
   Composer: Neil Sedaka
   Performed by: Neil Sedaka
   Year: 1961

P) Julia J. Austin

Q) "Stepford Wife" from the Movie *The Stepford Wives*
   Genre: Thriller/Horror
   Director: Bryan Forbes
   Cast: Paula Prentiss, Katharine Ross, Tina Louise, Mary Stuart Masterson, Peter Masterson, Nanette Newman, Patrick O'Neal, William Prince, Carol Rossen, Dee Wallace Stone
   Year: 1975

R) "The needs of the many outweigh the needs of the few, or the one." Quote from the Movie *Star Trek The Wrath of Kahn*
   Genre: Science Fiction
   Director: Nicholas Meyer
   Cast: William Shatner, DeForest Kelley, Leonard Nimoy, James Doohan, Walter Koenig, George Takei, Nichelle Nichols, Bibi Besch, Merrit Butrick, Paul Winfield, Ricardo Montalban and Introducing Kristie Alley as Saavik.
   Year: 1982

S) "SHMILY" by Laura Jeanne Allen (c)
1998, From, *Chicken Soup for the Couple's Soul* by Jack Canfield, Mark Victor Hansen, Mark and Chrissy Donnelly and Barbara De Angelis, Ph.D.
Publisher: Health Communications, Inc., January 1999, ISBN: 1558746463
(Or search "SHMILY" on the internet)

T) "You Don't Bring Me Flowers"
Medium: Song
Composers: Alan and Marilyn Bergman
Performed by: Neil Diamond and Barbara Streisand
Album: Early Classics
Year: 1978

Index

A

affirmations, 30, 31
alcohol, 5, 8, 9
anger, 43, 44, 46, 105, 107
attitude, 29-31, 78, 79, 93, 94, 115, 117, 119
    bad attitude, 94
    loving attitude, 46
    negative attitude, 30, 31
    nonchalant attitude, 121
    permissive attitude, 42
    positive attitude, 30, 31
    reactionary attitude, 112

B

behavior, 45, 60, 105, 124
    horrid behavior, 46
    juvenile behavior, 107
    loving behavior, 45
    obsessive-compulsive behavior, 80
    selfish behavior, 110
    sexual behavior, 95
Bible, 11, 37, 40, 41, 43, 85, 104, 111, 112, 115, 119, 125, 130

C

child, 39, 71, 110
children, 32, 42, 43, 68, 70, 71, 83, 84, 86, 88, 103, 104, 109, 127
Christian, 40, 41, 83-85, 119
Christianity 40, 41, 83
Clayton, John, 41
compatibility, 67, 68, 72, 78, 84, 86, 89, 90, 94, 98, 118, 129
communicate, 105,
communication, 105, 108, 111
confidence, 14-16
counting the cost, 96

D

dairy products, 19
diet, 5, 18, 21,
don't let yourself go, 108,

E

Ephesians, 111
ethnic background, 81
exercise, 21-23, 33, 34, 70, 71, 109, 126

F

family, 34, 68-70, 72-75, 84, 96
    family background(s) 74,
    family finances 123
    family relationships 104
    his family 68-70, 84
    my family 32, 46

your family 68, 69, 74, 84, 123
finances, 75, 123
financial, 123, 126
food, 6, 18-20, 48, 57, 78, 79, 108, 129
forgive(ness), 13, 126
friends , 3, 4, 33, 38, 41, 46, 51, 58, 59, 68-70, 77, 111
friendship, 58

G

goals, 32, 33
God, 7, 14, 34, 35, 38-41, 48, 49, 83-85, 88, 104, 125, 126

H

happy, 2, 3, 7, 11-13, 18, 25, 31, 40, 49, 52, 67, 71, 85, 86, 94, 113, 124, 125, 127, 129, 130
    happy marriage, 52, 108, 125,
    happy relationship 11, 17, 108,
health, 4, 8, 17, 21-23, 31, 34, 57, 78, 79,
healthier, 20, 31,
healthy, 1, 11, 15-18, 29, 40, 49, 67, 111, 124,
honest, 1-3, 11, 25, 29, 46, 47, 62, 67, 79, 95, 116, 120
husband, 46, 51, 57, 65, 72, 73, 78, 80, 81, 84, 85, 90-92, 94, 95, 97, 104, 105, 107-122, 124, 125, 127-131,

I

improvement, 1, 10, 12, 15-17, 28, 38, 57, 103
insecure, 17

J

jealous, 11, 12, 62, 123-125

K

L

Lewis, C.S., 40
lifestyle, 70, 72, 74, 75, 77,
love, 11-15, 29, 36, 39, 47, 51, 52, 58, 62, 66, 68-74, 76-83,
    95, 97-99, 112, 113, 116, 117, 119, 121, 122, 124, 125,
    129, 131, 132

M

makeup, 25, 26, 108, 109
microwave oven, 19, 20

N

negative, 30, 31, 42, 43, 83, 94, 107
    negative attitude 30, 31
    negative frame of reference 10
    negative outlook 94

O

outlook on life, 1, 13, 30, 74, 93, 94
over weight, 3, 21, 61

P

personal habits, 79,
personality type, 91, 92
pets, 77, 78, 104
political views, 86, 88, 89
positive, 29-31, 43, 83, 94, 98, 105
    positive affirmations, 30, 31
    positive attitude, 30, 31

positive frame of reference, 9
positive outlook, 13
positive turning point, 28
practical tips to husbands and wives, 125, 126
pray, 84, 85, 118
prayer, 14, 85, 118
priorities, 33, 34, 104

Q

R

race, 81, 82,
relationship, 1, 17, 35, 40, 42, 50, 52, 69, 71, 72, 74, 76, 77, 79-81, 84-86, 93, 96-99, 105, 107, 109, 110, 111, 114, 115, 127
    dating relationship, 58, 71, 85, 99
    doomed relationship, 99
    family relationship, 104
    happy relationship, 11, 17, 49 & 50, 108
    healthy relationship, 1, 18, 49
    interracial relationship, 82
    lifelong relationship, 52, 58, 86, 113, 130
    lifetime relationship, 65, 68, 73 & 74
    long-term relationship, 1, 17, 33, 62, 79, 82, 98
    marriage relationship, 105, 118, 124, 129
    relationship with a man, 1, 11, 16, 17, 33, 49, 55, 62
    romantic relationship, 58
    successful relationship, 78, 86, 94
    unhealthy relationship, 99
    your relationship, 69, 77, 99, 105, 107, 110, 111, 118, 119, 121, 122, 124, 125, 127
religious beliefs, 82-84, 86
right person, 10, 52, 66, 99, 103
romance, 51, 52, 65, 127-129, 131
romantic, 58, 66, 131

Ross, Hugh, 41

S
security, 15-17
self-control, 42-44
self-esteem, 1, 15, 16, 21, 69
sense of humor, 89-91
sex, 50, 94-96, 113, 124, 128-131
sexy, 5, 8, 128
Shakespeare, 114, 116
spiritual, 82-84, 86, 118
spiritually, 40
stress(ed), 5, 8, 48, 60, 127
successful, 1, 25, 49, 52, 78, 82, 86, 94, 98, 108, 113

T

talc, 25

U
unhealthy, 99

V

W

Wurmbrand, Richard, 41

X

Y

Z